ADULT LEARNING AND SOCIAL DIVISION: A PERSISTENT PATTERN

Volume 2

Issues arising from the NIACE survey on
adult participation in learning 2002

Edited by

NAOMI SARGANT and
FIONA ALDRIDGE

niace

promoting adult learning

Published by the National Institute of
Adult Continuing Education (England and Wales)

Renaissance House, 20 Princess Road West,
Leicester LE1 6TP
Company registration no. 2603322
Charity registration no. 1002775

First published 2003

NIACE has a broad remit to promote lifelong learning
opportunities for adults. NIACE works to develop
increased participation in education and training,
particularly for those who do not have easy access
because of barriers of class, gender, age, race, language
and culture, learning difficulties and disabilities, or insufficient
financial resources.

NIACE's website is www.niace.org.uk

Cataloguing in Publication Data
A CIP record of this title is available from the British Library.

Designed and typeset by Boldface
Printed in Great Britain by Russell Press

ISBN: 1 86201 167 2

ADULT LEARNING AND SOCIAL DIVISION: A PERSISTENT PATTERN

Volume 2

Contents

Introduction vii
Professor Naomi Sargant, Honorary Research Fellow, NIACE

1 **Research agendas: present and future** 1
Professor Naomi Sargant, Honorary Research Fellow, NIACE

2 **Participating in adult learning: comparing the sources and applying the results** 12
Steve Leman, Principal Research Officer, Department for Education & Skills

3 **The benefits of learning** 23
Professor Tom Schuller, Dean of the Faculty of Continuing Education at
Birkbeck College and Co-director of the Wider Benefits of Learning Research Centre

4 **Social capital and lifelong learning: survey findings on the relationship
between sociability and participation** 32
Professor John Field, Director of Academic Innovation and Continuing
Education, University of Stirling

5 **Lifelong learning trajectories in Wales: results of the
NIACE Adult Learners' Survey 2002** 42
Dr Stephen Gorard, Reader at Cardiff University School of Social Sciences

6 **Changing and persisting patterns: the public and lifelong learning in Scotland** 56
Professor Maria Slowey, Director of Adult and Continuing Education,
University of Glasgow

7 **Learning in adult life in Northern Ireland: the turning of the tide?** 81
Professor John Field, Director of Academic Innovation and Continuing
Education, University of Stirling

8 **Match or mismatch: do the findings reflect the qualitative evidence?** 92
Veronica McGivney, Principal Research Officer, NIACE

Appendices   **99**

1   RSGB's omnibus survey and random location sampling method   99
2   A guide to socio-economic class   101
3   Notes on the tables   102
4   Analysis of weighted and unweighted samples   103
5   Regions   105
6   The questionnaire   106

Introduction

Professor Naomi Sargant,
Honorary Research Fellow, NIACE

Past research

The National Institute of Adult Continuing Education (NIACE) has made a long-term commitment to mapping the pattern of adult participation in formal and informal learning. In part, its focus on surveys of the general population has been prompted by the previous lack of any such overall data collected and held over the years by providers, particularly in respect of less formal provision. In part, however, it has been due to the recognition that adults learn when and where they can, sometimes through the workplace, in anti-social hours, often attending programmes designed for younger learners, and having to fit their studies into a complex web of other demands on their time.

Early surveys reach back to 1936 when W E Williams, the Secretary of NIACE's predecessor, The British Institute of Adult Education, and A E Heath undertook a postal survey of over 500 members of all adult classes from the most varied occupations and areas (Williams and Heath, 1936). In 1953, Ernest Green reported on a postal survey entitled *Adult Education: why this apathy?* answered by almost 2,000 people, again mainly adult students (Green, 1953). Joseph Trenaman, then Secretary of the BBC, undertook a related survey in 1955–57 researching attitudes of the general public in the London area to educational communications and ideas linking these to people's access to sources of information, and to the ways in which those various sources combine to influence attitudes (Trenaman, 1957).

The most comprehensive of the early surveys *Adult Education: adequacy of provision* was commissioned by the Department for Education and Science (DES) in 1966 and carried out by National Institute of Adult Education (NIACE's immediate predecessor) under a steering group chaired by the then Minister, Christopher Chataway, and prepared and edited by Edward Hutchinson, then Director of NIAE (NIAE, 1970). While this was not a national sample as such, it was described as 'much the most substantial study of its kind in the field of adult education in Britain'. It assembled the results of 3,549 interviews with non-participants and participants in non-vocational adult education courses in seven Local Education Authority areas in England and Wales. The Chairman of the Steering Group, Christopher Chataway MP went on to comment 'It has been particularly timely that, in advance of publication, the factual content could be put at the disposal of the Russell Committee and that assistance could be afforded to the

Planning Committee for the Open University. The Russell Committee did not in fact report until 1973 by which time the Open University had already produced its first, albeit atypical, group of graduates and set up a large student research project, funded by the Social Science Research Council (SSRC). William Van Straubenzee a subsequent Minister suggested that the OU was to be allocated much of the national budget for adult education which otherwise might have been spent on Russell's recommendations.

The next main stimulus for national research into adult learning came in the mid-seventies via the setting up by the 1976 Labour Government of the Advisory Council for Adult and Continuing Education (ACACE) under the Chairmanship of Richard Hoggart. The DES in support of this policy, committed the whole of its annual post-school research budget in 1979/80 to the education of adults, setting up a Steering Group which reviewed priorities and funded three inter-related adult projects: *Adults: their educational experience and needs* (ACACE, 1982), a social survey of the general adult population, *Choosing to learn* (Woodley *et al*, 1987) a study of adult learners in a wide variety of institutional contexts and an area study *Post-initial education in the North-West of England* (Percy *et al*, 1983).

These three projects were to be complemented in 1978 by the addition of a set of questions on post-school education and training to be included in the fourth sweep of the 1958 National Child Development Study (NCDS) whose participants would soon be coming of age. The laconic comment on the Committee Note 2AER(5)1 appears only too familiar: 'Unfortunately, questions relating to education in the leisure context have had to be dropped as the Department's share of the questionnaire is not as large as at one time seemed likely'.

Interest in 'lifelong learning' in the 1970s and 1980s was also increasing in North America as was interest in France in the differently labeled '*education permanente*' and '*formation continue*'. The OECD was at the same time proposing policies for 'recurrent education', but there was to be little large-scale research-based activity into the education of adults in the UK for another decade.

The current sequence of surveys

The first of the current sequence of surveys entitled *Learning and 'leisure'* (Sargant, 1991) was initiated by Alan Tuckett, appointed as Director of NIACE in 1988, to mark the demise of the Inner London Education Authority. The ILEA had made an especial and large commitment to encouraging adult learning in London in the 25 years of its existence and he was interested to see if it was possible to identify the effect of this contribution in terms of its impact on London as a 'learning society'. The timing of the survey happened to coincide with a determined attempt on the part of the then Government to suggest that adult learning could be easily divided into 'leisure' and vocational' – hence the title. This governmental view led to the unfortunate distinction between Schedule 2 and other courses embedded in the 1992 Further and Higher Education Act!

Two other key studies were commissioned in 1989 and 1993 by the Employment Department focusing specifically on work-related education and training and concentrating only on those people in the labour market, aged 16–54. These were *Training in Britain* (Training Agency, IFF Research Ltd, 1989) and *Individual commitment to learning* (Park, A., SCPR, 1994). Two further surveys are not discussed here, though they provide relevant background, *Employment in Britain* (Gallie and White, PSI, 1993) was limited to vocational training or education among employees and *Learning for a Purpose* (Sargant, 1993) mapped out participation in education and training among the main minority ethnic groups, since the overall surveys of the general population did not provide large enough samples of individual communities for detailed analysis.

The second national study, *What price the learning society?* (Braunholtz and Tuckett, 1994), was funded for NIACE by the then Employment Department and focused more closely on adult education and access to and the quality of local provision. The third study in 1996 was funded by the Department for Education and Employment (DfEE) and and included the first full study of participation in Northern Ireland, with national studies also of Scotland and Wales. Its report *The Learning Divide* (Sargant *et al*, 1997) provided the most comprehensive coverage so far of the United Kingdom and looking forward to devolution, contained essays focusing on the individual nations to be. Also in 1996, the DfEE commissioned the National Centre for Social Research (formerly SCPR) to further develop their work resulting in the first National Adult Learning Survey (NALS), discussed later.

The fourth and fifth large-scale NIACE studies in 1999 and 2002, funded by the European Social Fund, have, in the interests of comparability and trend data, utilized essentially the same questionnaire framework as the 1996 survey and Volume One of this publication discusses these trends in some detail. These studies have been complemented in intermediate years with smaller projects which have looked, for example, at health and sporting activities in relation to learning, as well as asking about participation in learning and future intentions to learn (Aldridge and Lavender, 2000; Aldridge and Tuckett, 2001; Aldridge, 2001; Aldridge, 2002).

The 2002 survey is the fifth of a sequence of more obviously comparable surveys commissioned by NIACE, and the third to include Northern Ireland. The recent sequence carried out every three years has been designed to look broadly at adult participation in education and training and has pursued a number of themes in a comparable way, though the emphases have changed as the social, educational and policy environment has changed.

The series of quantitative studies have been complemented by significant qualitative work into the factors affecting adult access to learning opportunities and into strategies for overcoming such barriers to access. The seminal work in the qualitative sequence was Veronica McGivney's 1990 study *Education's for Other People: Access to Education for Non-participant Adults* (McGivney, 1990). This has been followed by a number of other qualitative studies by her on non-participating groups such as women returners, excluded men and part-time and temporary workers.

There have been two other distinguishing features of the NIACE research strategy: firstly, the need to cover regional differences and provide more detailed analyses of sub-groups of the population; secondly, the task of mapping the learning activities of the whole community and not just those active in the labour force. Both of these require a large sample size and it is the reconciliation of these purposes within the available funding which has dictated NIACE's choice of research strategy to date. The decision to build on and extend the English Local Labour Force Survey (ELLSF) to 60,000 will certainly provide more adequate sample sizes for local areas in England. The issue of adequate comparisons between the four nations still remains an issue as will the coverage of those parts of the population outside the labour-market age groups.

Comparability in questioning

There is no one best way to ask a particular set of questions, but if it is desirable to make comparisons over time, there is an obvious merit in trying to keep to the same questions wherever possible. There has been a gradual broadening of the way in which questions about learning have been framed over the years and it worth setting the changes down in detail to remind people what questions have been asked and why and how they developed the way they have. It is always difficult to make comparisons between different surveys carried for different purposes by different organisations.

The 1980 ACACE research was designed in the context of that time, to try to include study in its broadest sense, whether full or part-time, whether at work or elsewhere, since the completion of full-time education. The question used in 1980 was:

> Have you done any kind of study, learning or practising, part-time or full-time, at work or elsewhere since you completed your full-time education?

The 1990 survey re-used the 1980 question but added a question designed to elicit more information about informal learning, along the lines of the theories implicit in the work of Allen Tough (1971) and discussed in some detail in *Learning and 'leisure'* (Sargant, 1991)

> Are you studying currently, or have you done any kind of study, learning or practising, part-time or full-time, at work at home, with friends or in a club – for example cooking, how to use a computer, photography etc?

> Are you trying to learn about anything else at the moment, or trying to teach yourself anything, at work, at home, with friends or in a club – for example, cooking, how to use a computer, photography etc?

The 1994 MORI survey for NIACE adapted the first question slightly, asking about 'classes' rather than 'study' and did not add the supplementary question. Its phrasing was:

> Are you studying currently, or have you done any kinds of classes or learning, part-time or full-time, since you completed your full-time education, either at work or elsewhere?

The fieldwork for the SCPR study, *Individual commitment to learning*, published in 1994 in fact preceded the MORI poll and in its report describes its relationship to the 1990 survey in some detail. It produced a higher proportion engaged in learning than the 1990 survey and attributed this to 'variations in the ways in which the two surveys questioned respondents about learning'.

> Although the 'Individual commitment' survey took NIACE's definition of learning as its starting point, it structured key questions on learning in a different way. Namely respondents in the 'Individual commitment' survey were given a more detailed description of what was meant by learning and were taken through this description in a more methodical and structured manner than was possible in the NIACE survey. Through this it was hoped that respondents would have more time to consider whether they had undertaken any of the activities described as examples of learning. (Park A, 1994)

The SCPR survey did in fact produce appreciably more learning episodes, particularly of shorter vocational learning than the 1990 survey. Unlike the NIACE surveys, which use shorter sets of questions placed on omnibus questionnaires in order to produce large sample sizes, the SCPR survey was an 'ad hoc' survey, with 150 questions and 1400 respondents. The question SCPR developed in 1993 read as follows:

> This card describes the sort of learning people might do. Could you read the card please while I go through it with you. As the card says, learning can mean practising, studying or reading about something. It can also mean being taught, instructed or coached. This is so you can develop skills knowledge or abilities or understanding of something. Learning can also be called education or training. You can do it regularly (each day or each month) or you can do it for a short period of time. It can be full or part-time, done at home or at work, or in another place like a college. Learning does not have to lead to a qualification. We are interested in any learning you have done whether or not it was finished.

NIACE agreed to adopt the SCPR questioning for its next survey in 1996, and found that despite the use of the same question, the results of the surveys did appear to cover somewhat different territories though to a lesser extent than in earlier surveys. These differences are discussed in more detail in *The Learning Divide* (Sargant *et al*, 1997). Of course these surveys are three years apart in time. What is imponderable is the effect of the focus of the SCPR survey on vocational and work-related learning compared with the more general perspective on adult learning taken by NIACE, and whether or not the difference in the way the questionnaire and the actual leading question could have had an effect.

The SCPR survey was designed to focus on work-related learning, used the broader question, and did clearly pick up more short work-related episodes apparently omitted from NIACE surveys. At the same time many people studying for longer time periods are also studying for work-related reasons and may have been missed out of the SCPR survey. The conclusion may well be that both surveys underestimated the total quantity of current learning. Certainly the continued attempt to separate work-related learning from other forms of learning continues to cause statistical and inferential difficulties particularly in respect of future intentions to learn.

The complexity of issues arising from these earlier surveys led the DFEE to commission the National Centre for Social Research (NCSR) to carry out further development work on the optimum structure for, what is now called, the National Adult Learning Survey (NALS), the fieldwork for which took place in Spring 1997 (Beinart and Smith, 1998). NCSR developed interesting and more complex questionnaire approaches, which make direct comparison with the NIACE sequence of surveys difficult, though the general pattern of findings tells much the same story. NALS utilises very detailed sequences of question-probing and distinguishes taught learning and self-directed learning. Their large initial sample has also been used as the basis for a valuable follow-up study (La Valle and Fince, 1999).

After discussion, the decision taken was that it was not sensible to change the NIACE questionnaire again significantly for the 1999 and 2002 surveys, but that it was better to maintain the same questionnaire as closely as possible in order to be clear about bench-marking and other comparison measures as new government policies come into effect and to provide trend data over time, crucial in the short timeframes of government. The responses to the questionnaire has shown it to be reliable over the last three surveys, despite both a necessary change of agency from the Gallup Poll to RSGB, and a move to computer-based personal interviewing from personal interviewing. The value of this stability is demonstrated in Volume One, which has focused on making appropriate comparisons over the last three surveys in respect of overall participation rates and patterns of learning. The first volume also provides interesting comparisons between the original ACACE survey and the later ones over the last three decades in respect of leisure patterns and the use of cultural and community facilities.

A note on the contributors and contributions to this volume

In order to enrich the value of the surveys, researcher colleagues involved with NIACE were invited to join in a planning seminar for the 2002 survey, suggesting aspects of the research in which they were particularly interested and some ways in which the survey could be added to and strengthened without affecting its basic comparabilities. The contributions in this volume stem from their interest and commitment and we are grateful to them for their collaboration.

Chapter Two entitled *Participation in adult learning: comparing the sources and applying the results* by Steve Leman (Principal Research Officer, Department for Education & Skills), makes the vital bridge between the NIACE survey and other research sources, particularly the National Adult Learning Survey (NALS) commissioned by the Department for Education & Skills and its predecessor bodies. He considers the relationship between the surveys: their definition of learning, their target populations, their methodologies and the role and influence of such surveys in policy-making. His detailed description of the NALS series of questions about different forms of taught learning and self-directed learning follows on helpfully from the history of the NIACE and SCPR questions outlined earlier in this chapter.

In summary, Leman suggests, that 'the argument is that the variation between the results of different surveys flow from issues of scope – target population, definition of learning reference period – and of methodology, especially the different ways of asking questions about participation'. He notes that 'the NALS definition of learning has been incorporated into the Labour Force Survey. This allows us to draw on a much larger sample, and estimate participation by Local Education Authority area and by Learning and Skills Council local office area. It will enable better tracking of groups who are local priorities for widening participation.'

This move is extremely valuable in extending the local and regional scope of the survey. Issues which may also repay further attention are: the effect of the separation of job-related training from other leisure or education classes, (which are only asked in relation to the last four weeks), the continued inclusion of very short training episodes in the work-place and the breadth of the definition of learning ranging from the inclusion of 'learning how to drive' as a 'taught course' at the one extreme and 'reading a book or a journal' as 'self-directed learning' at the other.

NIACE has always taken the view that the distinction between taught and self-directed learning is not easy to maintain. An increasing number of people are studying part-time, sometimes using open or distance learning materials, and may do their study in more than one place. It is not clear at what stage open learning, using resource materials which are designed to be learner-centred and used for independent learning, should be classified as taught or non-taught courses. Similarly informal learning may well be recognized through accreditation of prior experience/learning schemes, though there has not been enough contemporary longitudinal work on informal learning and its role as a gateway to continuing learning to understand its significance.

Leman identifies a demanding set of questions on which more information is still needed and suggests that longitudinal work may be necessary to answer some of them. In this respect, the setting up of the Centre for Research on the Wider Benefits of Learning described by Tom Schuller in Chapter Three is encouraging as is the increasing focus on adults by the Centre for Longitudinal Studies. The original 1958 NCDS cohort, now part of the Centre's remits, is in the prime of its adult learning life!

In his chapter, *The benefits of learning*, Professor Tom Schuller, Dean of the Faculty of Continuing Education at Birkbeck College and one of the co-directors of the Centre for Research on the Wider Benefits of Learning reports on the setting up of the Centre, its brief and the breadth of thinking behind its work so far. In a challenge to the existing focus on participation issues, he suggests a number of explanations for the lack of focus on outcomes, not least that adult educators 'tend to take it for granted that participation is what counts, since adult education is self-evidently a good thing'. Another and more comfortable explanation, but a particular problem for both researchers and policy-makers, is the longer time frame required for some outcomes to be realized. Typically in current participation studies, many learners may increase their confidence quite early on in their studies, but will not necessarily yet have completed their studies, let alone achieved more instrumental and longer-term goals such as promotion or job-change. He concludes by considering some of the benefits and changes the 2002 survey reported relating them to the areas of interest to the Centre's work. This leads him to raise, finally, the key difficulty of 'tracing causal relations', a particularly difficult issue in social science research.

'Cause and effect' is also an issue for Professor John Field, Director of Academic Innovation and Continuing Education, University of Stirling in Chapter Four on *Social capital and lifelong learning*. He is particularly interested in people's patterns of social interaction and associations and their linkage with learning. His chapter draws on the work of Robert Putnam on social capital (Putnam, 2000). 'The core idea of social capital is the suggestion that people's connections have value. They allow people to cooperate for mutual benefit, and gain access to resources that they can then use.' Do people who engage in social activities more also engage in learning more? This idea bears similarity to Bourdieu's ideas in the 1970s in relation to cultural and educational capital, and it is interesting that these are now reappearing in the current discourse about social inclusion.

Field suggests that we might expect that people who have very active social lives full of leisure activities, would have less time to be adult learners. He works systematically through cross-analyses of the data both about learning and various types of social association, demonstrating that the opposite is the case: there is a very strong link between connectedness and learning: 'those who engage most in socializing are more likely than average to be learners.' He pursues interesting differences between leisure activities which are home-based and individual e.g. gardening and needlecrafts and those which involving interaction with others, finding lower levels of learning only with those engaged in more solitary pursuits.

Asking 'should we ban gardening and encourage adultery?' he suggests that 'if policy-makers want to promote adult learning and invest in community building, the evidence suggests that they should see these goals as clearly linked together… Strong communities are full of learners and learning communities are full of active citizens.' Finally, this leads him to the dangers of isolation and to the growing recognition of the learning and digital divide. People who are not as active as learners tend to be more isolated. 'Isolation may be as, if not more, common in urban estates where relationships have broken down…' than in rural areas. For those interested in urban renewal these are suggestive messages and well worth pursuing further by researchers.

Chapters Five, Six and Seven focus on what the survey says about Wales, Scotland and Northern Ireland respectively. The Welsh sample was boosted to 1,000 interviews and the main headline findings on participation for Wales have been published separately in a bi-lingual text and are not repeated here (Aldridge and Horrocks, 2002). In his chapter Dr Stephen Gorard, Reader at Cardiff University School of Social Sciences, reminds the reader that levels of participation and attainment have been traditionally lower in Wales than in the UK as a whole and then focuses particularly on comparisons between learners and non-participants.

In previous work on participation in lifelong learning, Gorard and colleagues had drawn both on a large-scale study of individual patterns of participation in lifelong learning and also on the oral history of the South Wales Coalfield Archive (Gorard, Fevre and Rees, 1999). Their work suggested that most of the factors that predict future participation in lifelong learning are already in place by the time children start primary school, and that only about 15% of the likelihood of lifelong learning is explained by what happens after they leave primary school. He uses a wide range of variables in stages ranging from birth and demographic variables, to language and access to technologies to establish lifelong learning trajectories. He concludes 'that whether or not an individual participates in learning is a life-long pattern, already presaged at school-leaving age, and intrinsically related to long-term social, economic and educational factors.

Gorard has also continued to be interested in the potential of ICT and of projects such as the UfI and virtual colleges to reach across traditional barriers to non-participants. However, he notes 'that evidence is mounting that non-participants are not especially deterred by traditional barriers such as time, cost, travel and lack of initial qualification but by the role of long-term socio-economic background characteristics, especially the influence of the family'. Access to ICT, he argues, also continues to be largely patterned according to (such) long-term factors and is therefore a proxy for the other more complex social and economic factors that pre-date it rather than as a direct contributory factor in itself.

It is necessary to note here that the digital divide is not the cause of the learning divide. The learning divide pre-dates it. However, as the 2002 survey makes clear, the information divide of which the digital divide is one part, is likely to increase the learning divide.

Chapter Six entitled *Changing and persistent patterns: the public and lifelong learning in Scotland* is contributed by Professor Maria Slowey, Director of Adult and Continuing Education, University of Glasgow. She identifies the relevant issue as the relationship between participation and learning. If 'participation does not necessarily equate with learning, and if our main interest is in learning, why do we care so much about analysing patterns of participation?' She answers her own question firmly, reminding us that while participation may not be a sufficient condition for learning it is a necessary one! More important she suggests, is that 'participation in education continues to be associated with important economic, social and personal benefits' and that we need to know who benefits from the perspective of equity.

Scotland has typically attached more importance to initial education than England though this has not automatically been carried over to lifelong learning. Slowey considers this issue and then goes on to analyse in detail the differences in participation and patterns of learning between Scotland and the UK as a whole. She concludes by outlining a number of interesting patterns in the data from Scotland, which she believes, require further explanation. These include the significance of the workplace; the existence of intergenerational inequalities and the persistence of social class and initial education background in shaping opportunities and attitudes to learning; and the significant inequalities in the level of support available to women compared to men. The findings also describe a situation in which although there has been significant growth in overall levels of participation, despite a generous definition of learning, one third still say that they have not participated since leaving full-time education. The policy implications of both this and the impact of current learning on future intentions to learn are also considered by Slowey to be key issues requiring more detailed investigation.

Chapter Seven is again contributed by Professor John Field, who had also contributed a chapter on Northern Ireland in 1997, when the Northern Ireland sample was boosted to 500 interviews. In the 2002 survey, resources were not made available for a boosted sample. Field therefore regards the findings as a prelude to further, more systematic investigation in the future, rather than viewing them as unambiguous evidence of patterns of participation.

In 2002, the survey findings suggest a significant rise in adult participation in Northern Ireland on previous years, providing the first evidence of any convergence between Northern Ireland and the rest of the UK. Field comments "although it is not possible to explain with confidence precisely why this shift has occurred, it has taken place at a time when policy makers have taken a number of steps to promote lifelong learning. For those who take the view that there is a direct connection between lifelong learning and the prosperity and social cohesion of a society, this is a very positive message."

The findings also confirm that the pattern of learning in Northern Ireland shows a number of distinct features, which contrast with the other UK nations. In particular, Field argues that the extent to which people in Northern Ireland are embracing the Internet as a way of accessing goods and services, suggests that considerable potential exists for new technologies to be of enormous significance in making online learning available to remote and rural communities and to those working in small firms and family enterprises.

Field concludes by identifying a number of continuing weaknesses to be tackled such as limited opportunities for workplace learning, poor take-up of vocational qualifications, the balance between the interests of learners and the labour market, and the inability of careers advisory services to engage effectively with adults. He also highlights a number of important strengths to be built upon – including positive attitudes towards learning, the high value placed upon informal sources of information and the strong benefits that learners associate with their learning.

Finally, in Chapter Eight Veronica McGivney raises important methodological issues concerning the limitations of survey research particularly in relation to understanding and measuring informal learning. She suggests that in qualitative studies, no matter how broad the definition of learning is, some people fail to mention more informal activities 'because they do not regard them as *proper* or *serious* learning'. She makes a similar point in relation to the use of the word 'subject' suggesting that some things that people are learning about or to do would not suggest themselves to people as 'subjects' and that this may again result in an under-reporting of the amount of informal learning.

Similarly she suggests that the wording and the placing of the questions about cultural activities are in themselves class-biased and may reinforce perceptions of learning and cultural activities as something that other people and social classes do. This links in with some of the social capital questions discussed by John Field in Chapter Four.

She comments on the increasing interest and research into informal learning and its relationship to formal learning, and the need for more research into this. It is clearly desirable to understand the nature and extent of informal learning and its role in relation to more formal learning. It is the increment of new learners that is the focus of the national targets. To put it into perspective, this may be, in any one year 1% or 200,000 learners. It is, of course, more difficult to try to measure it quantitatively, particularly when people do not define it as such themselves! Most qualitative research is, after all, focusing on non-learners, who by definition will offer quite different reasons for learning than will existing learners. And many people who are already learning formally are also learning something else informally.

References

ACACE (1982) *Adults: their educational experience and needs*, Leicester, ACACE

Aldridge, F. (2001) *Divided by language: a study of participation and competence in languages in Great Britain undertaken by NIACE*, Leicester, NIACE

Aldridge, F. (2002) *Sport: a leap into learning?*, Leicester, NIACE

Aldridge, F. and Lavender, P. (2000) *The Impact of Learning on Health*, Leicester, NIACE

Aldridge, F. and Tuckett, A. (2001) *Winners and losers in an expanding system: the NIACE survey on adult participation in learning*, Leicester, NIACE

Aldridge, F. and Horrocks, N. (2002) *Towards a learning future: the NIACE Dysgu Cymru survey on adult participation in learning in Wales*, Cardiff, ELWa

Beinart, S. and Smith, P. (1998) *National Adult Learning Survey 1997*, Sheffield, DfES

Braunholtz & Tuckett (1994) *What price the learning society?*, Leicester, NIACE

Gallie, D. and White, M. (1993) *Employee Commitment and the Skills Revolution*, PSI, London

Green, E. (1953) *Adult Education: why this apathy?*, London, Allen and Unwin

La Valle, I and Fince, S. (1999) *Pathways in Adult Learning*, London, DfEE

McGivney, V (1990) *Education's for Other People: access to education for non-participant adults*, Leicester, NIACE

NIAE, (1970) *Adult Education: adequacy of provision*, London, NIAE

Park, A. (1994) *Individual commitment to learning: individuals' attitudes*, Sheffield, Department of Employment

Percy, K. *et al.* (1983) *Post-initial education in the North West of England*, Leicester, ACACE

Putnam, R. D. (2000) *Bowling Alone: The collapse and revival of American community*, Simon and Schuster, New York

Sargant, N. (1991) *Learning and Leisure: a study of adult participation in learning and its policy implications*, Leicester, NIACE

Sargant, N. (1993) *Learning for a Purpose*, Leicester, NIACE

Sargant, N. and Aldridge. F. (2002) *Adult Learning and Social Division: a persistent pattern – the full NIACE survey on adult participation in learning 2002* Volume 1, NIACE, Leicester

Sargant, N. with Field, J., Frances, H., Schuller, T. and Tuckett, A. (1997) *The Learning Divide: a study of participation in adult learning in the United Kingdom,* Leicester, NIACE

Tough, A. (1971) The Adult's Learning Projects: A fresh approach to theory and practice in adult learning, Toronto, Ontario Institute for Studies in Education

Training Agency (1989) *Training in Britain: a study of funding, activity and attitudes,* London, HMSO

Trenaman, Joseph (1957) 'Education in the Adult Population, Part 1', in *Adult Education,* 30(3), pp.216–224

Williams W. E. and Heath, A.E. (1936) *Learn and Live: The Consumers' View of Adult Education,* London, Methuen

Woodley, A. *et al.* (1987) *Choosing to learn: adults in education,* Milton Keynes, Society for Research into Higher Education and the Open University Press

CHAPTER ONE

Research agendas: present and future

Professor Naomi Sargant, Honorary Research Fellow, NIACE

Participation as a continuing research issue

The sequence of national surveys described in these volumes has established the importance of participation as a key element of research in the field of adult learning, and ensured that such research is recognised as important by government. The 1997 *National Adult Learning Survey* (Beinart and Smith, 1998) was a development from the SCPR (Park, 1994) survey discussed earlier and sought particularly to understand informal learning, workplace based learning and non-participation. Information from these early studies was instrumental in the formulation of the idea of a learning participation target, and while the nature of the targets is developing, the government is committed to continuing research in order to measure their attainment. The setting up of the Learning and Skills Council (LSC) and its local arms has added impetus to this work and the extension of the English Local Labour Force Survey (ELLFS) to cover local LSC areas using the same questionnaire is much to be welcomed.

With devolution and the growth of regional government, it will continue to be necessary to look in detail at regional and local differences, since these may raise issues, among others, of access and equity. However, the ELLFS is just that, and only covers England. Larger sample sizes are also needed regularly in the other nations and it will be important for national surveys to include some common core of comparable information in order to make useful comparisons across the UK. Similarly if local LSCs want to commission more detailed local studies, it will be desirable to include a common core of comparable information in order to enable useful comparisons to be made across the UK at local level. This was an important lesson made clear in the numerous attempts to monitor, compare and transfer good practice through the TEC national network.. It is to be hoped, that the LSC, which is one organisation, will make more coherent the desire for new knowledge about participation across the country.

It is also necessary to understand more about the participation and learning needs of ethnic minority groups. A start on this was made in *Learning for a Purpose* (Sargant, 1993) a NIACE-led study of participation in education and training by adults from different ethnic minority groups. Issues of particular interest in that survey related to the amount and nature of informal learning, ESOL needs and recognition of overseas qualifications. The 2001 census should provide an up-to-date picture of the size and scatter of these groups in the UK and indicate whether or not the

ELLFS will provide an adequate framework to cover England and if so what is an appropriate strategy for the other nations. A similar need either for a large sample or for more purposive sampling also arises with special groups such as older people or those with learning or other disabilities.

Field (1999), in an article on participation comments on the current tide of debate over lifelong learning and also confirms the importance of participation as a topic for research. He draws attention to the wider community of policy-makers, managers, teachers and learners both in Britain and overseas who are now concerned with the issues of lifelong learning. He goes on to comment:

> 'Within this wider shift, one topic stands out from the others: participation. As lifelong learning has moved up the policy agenda, the question of who participates and who does not (and why) is posed ever more sharply. Research will also want to examine why this is such an important issue for policy-makers.'

He argues that Britain is now relatively well-served in the volume and quality of research about participation but goes on to suggest that this raises policy issues implicit in the suggestion that '*everyone* must constantly acquire new skills and knowledge in order to adapt and innovate in their present job or to enhance their employability should they need a new job…the more this argument is accepted by government and others, the wider the gulf between the "knowledge-rich" and "knowledge-poor" so that considerable efforts have to be devoted to social inclusion strategies'. This proposition parallels many of the arguments put forward in the NAGCELL (National Advisory Group for Continuing Education and Lifelong Learning) reports and in the research evidence that focuses on social inclusion and the information divide (NAGCELL, 1998; SEU, 1999; SEU, 2000).

Field (1999) in the same article comments usefully on other needs and omissions: firstly the omission from research of what he calls 'coerced' learning: the learning which is required by employers or professions, whether the learners want to do it or not such as health and safety; secondly, the need to understand better why some people define themselves firmly as non-learners; thirdly the effect of focusing on the accumulation of individual educational capital rather than the larger returns to social capital. The 2002 survey has been able to make a modest contribution to the first of these, identifying 6% of people who did not choose their learning. It is encouraging that an analysis of benefits of learning found that this group of learners are most likely to have been helped or expect to be helped in their current job (29%). However the findings also suggest that they may be less likely to experience some of the wider benefits of learning that are so valued by other learners, such as increased self-confidence, meeting new people and enjoying leaning more. The survey report and Field's own chapter on social capital demonstrate the inter-relationship between individual educational capital and access to social and cultural capital: the challenge is how to widen the virtuous circle.

The current national research scene as it relates to lifelong learning

Though lifelong learning is still high on the national agenda, its priorities are not now as clearly and broadly articulated as they were at the time of *The Learning Age* Green Paper (DfEE, 1998). There have been five different Ministers in charge of lifelong learning since the 1977 election. While the Learning and Skills Council has an Adult Committee its policies have received little media coverage and perhaps inevitably most attention is focused on the young, up-skilling and, increasingly, work-force development.

Some benefit has accrued from the increased focus by government on social science research. David Blunkett both castigated and encouraged social researchers, including educational researchers, in a key speech on the relationship between social science and government.

"I believe passionately that having access to the lessons from high quality research can and must vastly improve the quality and sensitivity of the complex and often constrained decisions we, as politicians, have to make."

David Blunkett. ESRC Lecture: *Influence or irrelevance: can social science improve government?* 2 February 2000

Attention has increasingly been focused on the need for more quantitative capacity in UK social science and this has been linked with the adoption of an evidence-based approach to research for policy-making, similar to that utilised in clinical research. It is encouraging that the ESRC is taking a number of steps to improve research methods capacity, notably by setting up a new five-year £4 million Research Methods Programme and producing new Postgraduate Training guidelines requiring training in the use of both qualitative and quantitative data.

While educational research shares some the difficulties of social science research in general, it faces some specific difficulties, particularly in relation to research into adult learning. A somewhat political issue is that for most people, teachers, parents, politicians and administrators, education is still synonymous with schooling. Adult learning is an afterthought. The field of educational research is similarly dominated by the interests of schools, schooling and its providers and with the exception of higher education has rarely been extended to the education of adults. This dominance has carried through to funding research, assessment panels and other decision-making structures. It has led and still leads to the omission of proper consideration of the needs of adult and lifelong learning.

A significant example is the National Educational Research Forum established in September 1999 with the remit of providing strategic direction for education research and developing a national framework within which a coherent research programme relevant to policy and practice can be developed. Its follow-up papers *A Research and Development Strategy for Education: developing quality and diversity* (NERF, 2001) also identifies the need to expand research capacity.

Written at a macro level, it identifies five characteristics of an effective strategy all of which are generally relevant to any educational research, but none of which have anything particular to say about adult learning:

- A coherent set of objectives;
- A plan that will focus simultaneously on theoretical issues and those of practical relevance;
- Enhanced coordination and sustained resourcing to underpin the plan;
- Ways of understanding and assessing the impact of research;
- Methods for monitoring, evaluating and reviewing progress.

It suggests a Foresight Exercise specifically about education and a Standing Group to establish criteria for setting priorities. It recommends a regular national survey of practitioners and institutions' priorities and a forum of funders. Initial membership of the forum and its working groups included only one person specifically from the field of adult and lifelong learning. In its discussion of capacity, while it does include NIACE and the British Educational Research Association (BERA), it does not include the post-school research groupings SCUTREA , UCACE or SRHE and mentions lifelong learning only once.

More positively the document does recognise that educational research is located within, and draws on, many other disciplines requiring a broad range of methodologies, and may need to be multidisciplinary and move beyond "the polarised debate between quantitative and qualitative approaches".

All these recommendations are unexceptionable. What is unacceptable and a matter of great concern is that despite specific requests from NIACE and other professionals engaged in lifelong learning, the paper is still silent on the research needs of adult learning at a time when adults now form a larger population group than those in schooling and pose a number of quite different methodological problems. It is especially ironic that the closing sentence of the Strategy Paper looks forward to the OECD visit 'which will be conducting a review of education research' as an 'opportunity to review progress and identify future priorities'. In the event, the DfES Background Report (DfES, 2002) concentrated on 'pre-collegiate education and therefore their interview schedule arranged did likewise. While some of its general conclusions are of general interest, the inspectors note:

> "Our interviews and the DfES Background Report concentrated on pre-collegiate education. Our focus has thus been almost exclusively on pre-collegiate practice and policy. As a result the review provides very limited analysis of higher and adult education".
> (OECD, 2002)

Each time an opportunity such as this is missed, the needs of adult learning become more invisible. It would be interesting to know whether the decision to focus the background report for the OECD inspection only on schooling was a matter of omission or commission.

Issues in common across educational research

Educational research has, indeed, faced a number of difficulties over the years. First, most academic research in higher education is funded through and driven by academic disciplines, psychology, sociology, economics etc. and education is not a discipline as such, but rather an applied research area which needs to draw on each of these and some others. Second, disciplines tend to fight for territory and compete for resources rather than collaborate. Most disciplines favour or utilise particular research methodologies and are not generous about recognising other methods. 'My data are hard, your data are soft' is a typical criticism. For example, psychology uses experimental design, test and measurement and attitude scaling, among others and anthropology uses participant observation. Neither of these paradigms, nor that of illuminative evaluation, were of particular use to the Open University who had to develop sophisticated self-administered questionnaires to samples of learners studying on their own at home.

The large-scale sample surveys used in social and market research have been out of favour with academics partly for socio-political reasons and partly because they are too expensive and technical for most academics to mount. Individual academics researching on their own, whether psychologists or sociologists, can handle smaller sample sizes, focus groups, in-depth interviews with content analysis and ethnographic approaches more easily. Qualitative approaches have been particularly favoured for classroom and observational studies. The choice between qualitative and quantitative research needs to be taken rationally: the academic battleground over recent decades has been unhelpful and has played its part in reducing capacity and academic effectiveness.

Professor Bruce in the September 2002 ESRC newsletter (ESRC, 2002) writes eloquently on this issue about his own field of religion. He comments that when writing in 1989, he and a colleague had 'praised particularly the British tradition of detailed ethnographic studies of sects, cults and new religious movements. In the years since, my admiration for detailed case studies of religious groups has not faded, but I have become increasingly aware of a major weakness in … the sociology of religion generally: an unwillingness or inability to engage in the statistical analysis of large-scale quantitative data… Numbers are not everything, but they are something… I do not want to assert that quantitative studies of religion are better than ethnographic case studies, only that they are essential in two ways. First, without reliable large-scale data we may easily mistake the meaning of our case-studies…Second, large-scale data is necessary to test the plausibility of explanations based on case-studies.'

Education as an applied research area, needs to be able to employ a range of research techniques: to analyse a problem and choose the most appropriate technique to research that problem. Different research techniques should not be seen as in competition with each other. The move to evidence-based policy is helpful as it focuses on evidence which addresses the policy decision to be made, though its experimental origin stemming from clinical and medical research as well as the test-and-measurement 'agriculture-botany paradigm' is that of 'randomised control trials' and is not particularly suitable for uncontrollable adult learners or, with equity, for disadvantaged school children.

This matters in terms of research strategy and capacity since the key research issues in adult learning and the methodologies used are likely to be significantly different from those appropriate in closed classroom situations. While there is more potential linkage between techniques used in closed classrooms, whether it be in school or in further/higher education, increasing numbers of adults are studying in the workplace, at home, or through open/distance learning and have to be reached through sample surveys of learners by post or individual interview and not in controlled and observable environments. Informal learning is also likely to require new approaches. It may also not be ethical to offer some people opportunities and not others, whether chosen at random or not. Issues of curriculum and assessment are likely to require different approaches for adults than for the young.

In terms of capacity, the tradition of applied social research and its training, including most educational research, is weaker methodologically in the UK than it is in North America. Few academics have a strong research methods background. We lack the number of major non-profit applied social research agencies there are in the US. There is little interchange of professional staff between market and opinion research agencies and academic departments. Academics tend to underestimate the professional skills involved in questionnaire design, for example, and work on longer timetables. Social and academic researchers tend to look down on market researchers. Without external funding, few academics can afford the large data sets that are necessary for much applied educational and social research. The case for large-scale sample surveys has been weakened further by the fashion for focus groups which are increasingly used as a substitute for rather than a complement to quantitative research.

The dominant post-graduate research training paradigm, the three-year individual supervised research project has developed from the physical sciences, where the notion of working with the professor as part of a research team in a lab, or as a research apprentice is still the norm in medicine and the sciences. It is much less useful in the social sciences, where the analogy would be that of a consultant only learning about one illness, rather than a GP dealing with a variety of problems.

A vital issue in the social sciences is that there is no pressure to have a collective memory or agreement about what constitutes an advance in knowledge in the way that science and technology must. In science, a new finding or discovery is seen, evidenced, published and disseminated and then, typically built on by the next wave of researchers. This does not necessarily happen in the social sciences. As noted earlier, in social science there continue to be battles between disciplines, there are fashions in methods and theories, grounded theory, epistemology, *etc.* References over ten years old are old-hat even if they were seminal and have not been disproved. An example currently of the lack of connection is Gorard's work described in Chapter 5 which echoes the classic work on education and social mobility in the 1950s and 1960s carried out within by sociology (Glass, 1954) at LSE and then at Nuffield College, Oxford, and also pursued in relation to social mobility among Open University students (McIntosh *et al*, 1976).

The impact of the Research Assessment Exercise is not without guilt in this game-playing and is feeding the growth of social science journals covering even more specialist disciplines. And peer review tends to reinforce discipline-based boundaries!

What of the future?

More effort is now going into research into post-school education and it will be important to monitor its impact. The ESRC's Learning Society Research Programme directed by Frank Coffield has produced much valuable work, including Coffield's (2000) own text on Informal Learning. Field & Schuller (1999) in a helpful paper entitled *Investigating the Learning Society'* reviewed the programme, commenting, inter alia, that adult practitioners were in a minority among those involved in the programme. They identified a number of future research priorities that had emerged from the work so far, under seven headings:

- Definitions of the field
- Participation, distribution and change
- Learners' environments
- Learners' careers
- Time and money
- Complementarity and competition
- The knowledge base

It would be important to identify how far conclusions from this major programme have already fed into policy and into academic thinking, and in which areas research is continuing. The Learning Society and Teaching and Learning Research programme (ESRC) series contains research from a variety of disciplines and it will be interesting to see how far the knowledge base developed is capable of being synthesised, or if academics are interested in such a challenge.

Looking ahead, there are three promising developments, the new set of Research Centres set up under DfES auspices, the next round of the ESRC Teaching and Learning Programme (TLTP2) and the Research Strategy (2002–2005) of the Learning and Skills Research Centre (LSRC) under the Learning and Skills Development Agency with funding from the DfES and the LSC. The new set of DfES research centres are described elsewhere and Chapter 3 focuses on one of them. The LSRC sets out ambitious goals:

> "It aims to be an authoritative source of knowledge and ideas, informing and influencing the future development of a successful and sustainable system of post-16 learning, The LSRC will create a strong body of evidence from rigorous research, focused on creative,

critical and innovative thinking, and models for the long-term development of post-16 learning. The Centre will work to ensure that research has a strong and positive impact on the development of policy and practice."

They note that the LSRC is the first centre sponsored by the DfES to focus solely on post-16 learning and that four main factors have driven the Centre's initial strategy. These are:

- deep-seated problems that are relevant to policy development and practice in post-compulsory learning, e.g. social exclusion, disengagement from the democratic process;
- far-reaching trends that will need to be addressed to provide learning for the 21st century: e.g. globalisation, the communications revolution, demographic change, the implications of free trade and mobility of labour;
- government policies in moving towards a knowledge-based/learning society;
- research needs identified by existing users or practitioners.

The distinctive features, principles and values are unexceptionable, but written at a very general level and with all the right words. But, as with most good research, there will be few quick answers.

The Research Strategy identifies five programmes: 1) participation in post-compulsory learning; 2) vocational learning, skills and work; 3) developing learning and teaching; 4) the organisation of learning; 5) developing the work force for post-compulsory learning. Underpinning these programmes, they note, is a focused strategy designed to increase the impact of research, develop research methods, build research capacity and develop knowledge management systems. Described as the Building Effective Research strategy, it will focus on developing capacity and innovation. 'It will investigate how to enable impact and ensure that research evidence is clear, timely and used effectively for policy and practice'. To achieve this, as an applied researcher, is, of course, to find the Holy Grail!

This is not the place to examine the five programmes in detail and the texts make convincing arguments for each of the programmes, identifying for each topic, the first year's priority. Programme 1 will focus on the role brokers and intermediaries can play as enablers of participation. Programme 2 will focus on an effective VET system for the 21st century, enabling access and coherent routes to successful learning for individuals, employers and the economy. Programme 3 will focus on non-formal learning and its relationship to formal and work-based learning, including the impact of assessment regimes, and the challenges of assessing informal and e-learning. Programme 4 will focus on funding learning in the future, to include identifying what different groups of people think and do about financing their own and their families' learning; and what we can learn from other countries about the financing of learning. Programme 5 will focus on the leadership behaviours needed to create tomorrow's successful learners. Finally in respect of the overarching Building Effective Research strategy, the first year's work will focus on effective models of research impact.

Managing a programme of applied research on this scale with a tight timetable is a daunting project. It is not clear whether all the work is likely to be done in-house or whether some areas will be contracted out and some academic departments tend to work on longer time-scales. There are clearly likely to be issues of overlap with Phase III of the TLRP which has also been through a major consultation exercise with some of the same players. The next round of TLRP has £8 million plus to spend on post-compulsory education and training as a whole including higher and further education, community education, work-based learning (including continuing professional development) and lifelong/adult learning. 'Developing research capacity is a key objective of this phase!' Projects are due to start in June 2003 and the three themes identified are:

- Learners and learning
- Teachers, trainers and learning environments
- Learning communities

It is clear that there will be plenty of work in sight for anyone with a half-way decent CV in education or social science research methods. The challenge will be to ensure that these major programmes do not overlap unnecessarily and that appropriate linkages, networks and partnerships are set up at an early stage. The review commissioned in preparation for TLRP III from the Tavistock Institute should be helpful in this regard.

Paying lip-service to lifelong learning

The Learning Age: a renaissance for a new Britain (DfEE, 1998) gave encouragement that there would be a real move to an overall vision for lifelong learning which would ensure that people would be able to move in and out of appropriate educational opportunities at any age as they needed or as they wanted. The traditional barriers and battles between sectors and levels were to be removed. Five years later it is evident that this is not the case. Already the ESRC's prestigious TLRP programme (*sic*) 'will focus on teaching and learning in post-compulsory education and training *including higher and further education, community education, work-based learning (including continuing professional development) and lifelong/adult learning.*' While the breadth of educational activity to be included in their £8 million research programme is to be welcomed, lifelong learning no longer provides the overarching vision, but is on the margin as just another category grouped with traditional adult education.

It could be argued that terminology should not matter but the evidence is that it does. There have been continued attempts to find an acceptable term to distinguish between schooling or education for children and young people at the start of their lives and what might follow on from that initial education whether it finished at school, college or university. In the 1970s, while OECD favoured 'recurrent education', UNESCO preferred 'education permanente' and the US adopted 'lifelong learning', utilised particularly in relation to Mondale's ill-fated plans for Lifelong Learning. Debate in the UK was given impetus by the Open University's Report of its

Committee on Continuing Education (1976) chaired by Sir Peter Venables, and the setting up in 1977 by the then Labour Government of the Advisory Council for Adult and Continuing Education, chaired by Richard Hoggart.

This interest did not translate itself into government policy or financial commitment in the 1980s, though there were advances on the training and vocational education front (VET) which helped adults, mainly led by the MSC and its successor agencies under the leadership of Geoffrey Holland. Continuing education in the 1980s became coterminous with continuing professional development and the government's focus was on work-related education rather than on a more generous view of adult learning, with funding streams continuing to favour the young. The setting up of the ESRC's Learning Society programme in 1994 came as a significant breakthrough.

NB:

Field and Schuller (1999) commented on the explosion of public interest in lifelong learning in the second half of the 1990s, both among policy-makers and practitioners, and suggested that the language used in a number of countries 'was more or less distant from the older, more established discourses of adult and/or continuing education: notably the use of the term 'lifelong learning' and the phrase 'the learning society'. They went on to ask what the new language signalled for research: was it just a modish trend, a re-branding, or did it denote a more substantial change? Some people hoped for the latter. *successful terminology – not so scarey.*

However, looking across Europe, an increasingly important player in the field of adult learning, it is evident the different ways in which adult education, continuing education and lifelong learning are used and translated has more to do with language, culture and fashion than with deep educational or philosophical differences. What is still needed is a generic term which has general recognition and can be used to gain general support from the wide variety of stake-holders in adult learning, preventing individual interests being picked off in a way which weakens the overall cause. *still searching*

Lifelong learning does not yet appear to be a strong enough term to achieve this, even apart from the fact that for some it is taken to mean 'from cradle to grave'. Adult learning continues to be a helpful halfway term as it has shifted the focus on to the learner and away from the provider, and made it clear that it is the learner's motivation that determines whether learning is work-related and vocational or not, rather than the decision of the provider or the funder. It is too early to assess the impact of the Learning and Skills Councils on general adult and community provision locally. However, current policy priorities are not encouraging for general adult learning. Young people are back up the agenda, there is a renewed focus on skills with the Skills Strategy in planning, and the latest favoured term is workforce development, seen to be a key to employers involvement and running alongside the work of the new Sector Skills Councils.

It will be increasingly important to have cogent evidence of the wider importance of adult learning for an inclusive society and for active democracy.

References

Coffield, F. (ed) (2000) *The necessity of informal learning*, Bristol, Policy Press

Department for Education and Employment (1998) *The Learning Age: a renaissance for a new Britain*, London, HMSO

Department for Education and Skills (2002) Research and development in England: Background report prepared for the OECD review, DfES

Economic and Social Research Council (2002) 'The Book of Numbers' in *Social Sciences*, Issue 52, ESRC

Field, J. and Schuller, T. (1999) 'Investigating the Learning Society' in *Studies in the Education of Adults*, 31(1), Leicester, NIACE

Glass, D. (ed) (1954) *Social Mobility in Britain*, London, Routledge

McIntosh, N. *et al.* (1976) *A degree of difference*, SRHE

National Educational Research Forum (2001) *A Research and Development Strategy for Education: developing quality and diversity*, NERF

OECD (2002) *Educational Research and Development in England: Examiners' Report*, OECD

Open University (1976) *Report of the Committee on Continuing Education*, Milton Keynes, Open University

CHAPTER TWO

Participating in adult learning: comparing the sources and applying the results

Steve Leman, Principal Research Officer, Department for Education & Skills

This chapter compares the NIACE surveys with other sources, mainly the National Adult Learning Survey (NALS) commissioned by the Department for Education and Skills, and looks at the stability of the relationship. It examines what the surveys taken as a whole can tell us, and what they cannot. In summary the argument is that the variation between the results of different surveys on adult learning flow from issues of scope – target population, definition of learning reference period – and of methodology, especially the different ways of asking questions about participation. Finally the chapter outlines some ways in which research on participation, and on what influences it, has informed Government policy.

What is a "learner"?

Many adult learning experts argue that there is no such thing as a "non-learner". They have a point. All human beings learn from experience every day. On this basis, the "adult learning participation rate" is one hundred per cent. However, for reasons of relevance to policy our surveys only include instances where an adult has *deliberately* tried to learn something.

The NALS surveys ask a series of questions about the different forms of taught learning and self-directed learning. Taught learning includes courses meant to lead to qualifications or to develop skills for a job; tuition in driving, music-making, art, crafts, sport any practical skill; evening classes; working from a package provided by an employer or learning provider; and any other taught course, instruction or tuition.

Self-directed or non-taught learning includes studying for qualifications without taking part in a taught course; supervised training while doing specific tasks at work; keeping up to date with developments in one's field of work – for example, by reading books, manuals or journals or attending seminars; and any other attempt to improve knowledge or skill without taking part in a taught course.

---

[1] Vocational learning was defined as learning, either taught or self-directed, that was started to help with current or future work, paid or voluntary.

To capture the full breadth and diversity of learning experiences, we define an interviewee as a "learner" if any of these activities has been done during the previous three years. We also produce one-year estimates (providing quicker feedback on policy developments) which tend to be slightly lower, because the three-year reference period picks up "occasional" learners. Snapshot figures derived from administrative statistics, referring to learning done in a single month or week, are much lower still. A less inclusive definition of learning would also result in a lower figure.

In 2002 (Fitzgerald, Taylor and La Valle 2003, forthcoming), 76% of respondents had taken part in one or more learning activities in the previous three years. This represented an increase from the 1997 figure (74%). There have also been changes in participation in different types of learning:

- the proportion of taught learners has gone up: 58% of adults reported this type of learning in 1997 and 61% in 2002;
- over the same period participation in self-directed learning has increased, from 57% to 61%; and
- participation in vocational learning has risen from 67% in 1997 to 69% in 200 ; but
- by contrast, participation in non-vocational learning has gone down, from 30% in 1997 to 26% in 2002.

The NIACE surveys from 1996 to 2002 take a similarly broad and inclusive approach, including both taught and self-directed learning, done currently or in the last three years. Rather than using a series of prompts, the NIACE surveys provide a single statement of what is in scope. This defines learning as practising/studying/reading or being taught/instructed/coached, to develop skills, knowledge, abilities or understanding. The definition mentions various words – learning, education and training – that people may recognise as applying to their experiences. It makes clear that learning may occur at home or work as well as in venues like colleges; and that learning experiences still count if they do not lead to a qualification, or if they are unfinished. On this basis the 2002 NIACE survey, across the four UK nations, found a participation rate in current/recent learning (during the last three years) of 42%. The figure was 40% in both 1996 and 1999.

Since the NALS and NIACE definitions of learning are very similar in principle, it is at first sight puzzling that the participation rates diverge so widely: from around two in five in most of the NIACE surveys between 1996 and 2002, to around three-quarters in most of the NALS exercises between 1997 and 2002. The most likely explanation is the cumulative nature of the NALS procedure: respondents get ten opportunities, each prompted by a short question, to recognise experiences in their lives as episodes of learning. By contrast, in the NIACE surveys the respondent relates a single question to a fairly lengthy definition.

Although the two survey series give different absolute levels of participation, they are both useful as measures of trend over time. Both have been subject to apparent blips: NALS in 2000 when a dip in participation seems to be explained by a temporary change of research contractor. The 2001 NIACE survey showed a sharp rise, not sustained in 2002, that is not confirmed either by NALS or by the English Local Labour Force Survey (ONS 2002b) which includes learning questions closely modelled on the NALS methodology. Overall, both sources indicate a modest upward trend between the mid-1990s and the early years of this decade.

NALS has used the same definition over time except for the conflation of two categories of non-taught learning in 2000 only. The NIACE definition has been stable from 1996 to 2002. NIACE and its predecessor organisations deserve credit for evolving a broad, inclusive definition over the years. Earlier definitions, and the associated participation rates (NIAE 1970; ACACE 1982; Sargant 1991) included:

- 1970: Local Education Authority + Workers' Educational Association + HE extra-mural only
  – 8% current or within the last year
- 1980: study/learning/practising, at work or elsewhere, full or part time
  – 47% since completing full-time education
- 1991: as in 1980, plus informal learning
  – 36% in the last three years

What is an "adult"?

For the National Adult Learning Survey (Beinart and Smith1997; Blake and La Valle 2001; Fitzgerald, Taylor and La Valle 2003, forthcoming) our contractors interview individuals (6,500 in 2001 and 2002) in a representative sample of households in England and Wales. We capture precise information about age, permitting analysis according to different age bandings. There is no upper age limit in the 2001 survey, though many of the analyses – including the participation "headlines" in the published reports – focus on the 16–69 age range, for comparability with the 1997 figures. Nobody below the age of 16 is interviewed.

We also exclude anyone who is still in full-time education following on directly from school – for example, students in further or higher education – even if they took a gap year after school. This variable lower age limit reflects the present-day educational scene – full-time initial education can finish at any age between the end of compulsory schooling at 16 and, say, the late twenties for some doctoral students. We also capture demographic information including socio-economic group, household status, ethnicity, disability and level of highest qualification.

The dataset is lodged with the ESRC Data Archive, enabling independent analysis which can, if needed, use combinations of demographic criteria other than those in the published report.

Variations in participation

In the 2001 survey[2] the highest participation rates were found among adults in paid work. Eighty-nine per cent of full-time employees, 82 per cent of self-employed and 81 per cent of part-time employees had done some learning. Sixty-eight per cent of unemployed people and just over half (52 per cent) of those looking after the family reported some learning. The lowest participation figures were found among those outside the labour market: retired people (48 per cent) and those unable to work due to a health problem or disability (42 per cent).

Among adults with no qualifications, less than a third (31%) report doing some learning over a three-year period. Similarly, 55% who left initial full-time education with no qualifications had undertaken some learning, compared with 94% of those who left with a qualification above NVQ level 3. Participation ranges from 85 % in the least deprived wards to 63 % in the most deprived ones. Women (73%) are less likely than men (79%) to report some learning. Fifty-six per cent of people with a work-limiting disability reported some learning, as compared to 76% for the population as a whole. Participation in vocational learning tends to decline with age, but non-vocational learning remains stable, as shown by Figure 1 (Blake and La Valle 2001):

Figure 1: Learning by age – NALS 2001

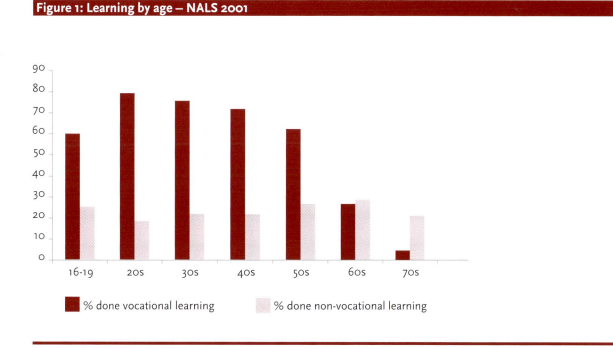

Among those with a household income of £31,200 or over, 91 per cent reported some learning; but only 53 per cent of those in the lowest income bracket (below £10,400). Socio-economic group has a strong influence, particularly on vocational learning:

---

[2] Apart from the headline figures cited above, most of the 2002 data are not yet in the public domain. The NALS 2002 report will be published in early 2003.

Table 1: Percentages of SEG groups reporting different types of learning

	All	Professional/ managerial	Other non-manual	Skilled manual	Semi-skilled manual	Un-skilled manual
	%	%	%	%	%	%
Any learning	80	88	85	70	71	53
Taught learning	62	70	69	48	54	32
Self-directed learning	64	77	67	55	50	33
Vocational learning	74	82	78	66	62	42
Non-vocational learning	25	27	29	19	20	16

Base: all respondents aged under 70 currently employed or self-employed or who have been in paid employment in the past 10 years
Source: Blake, M. and La Valle, I. (2001)

These patterns were described in the 1990s as a "learning divide" (Sargant 1997), and despite the modest overall increase in participation there has been little narrowing of the gap since then.

Why do adults learn?

The NIACE surveys ask the reasons for subject choices. Similarly, in DfES surveys we ask individuals for what purpose they undertook the learning. The broad categories are vocational and non-vocational. Vocational learning may be related to a current job, a future job or voluntary work, and learning started with one purpose can turn out to serve another. Someone starting a French course for a non-vocational reason – for example, to get more out of a holiday – could eventually use their language skills to sell goods or services to France in their work role.

Figure 2: Reasons for taught learning

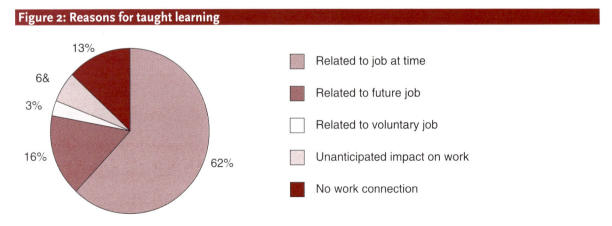

Base: all respondents aged under 70 who had done taught learning in the past three years
*The categories presented in the table are mutually exclusive and represent the main reason for which the selected learning episode was done.
Source: Blake, M. and La Valle, I. (2001)

What the surveys tell us, and what they do not

From the NIACE and NALS surveys we have learned a great deal about the characteristics of individual learners, the economic or other purposes of the learning they undertake, and the nature of the learning itself. However, we still lack full information on:

- progression from "first bite" provision to formal, accredited learning;
- the proportion of 'non-learners' who become 'learners' (and vice-versa) and what drives these processes;
- movements between non-taught and taught learning, between non-vocational and job-related and learning and between different levels of learning;
- progress in attainment for different groups and in different circumstances – which would illuminate issues such as whether childcare provision for adult learners should be a universal entitlement or a targeted programme;
- medium-term economic outcomes of learning – employability and earnings;
- returns to the less formal types of learning, such as recreational courses undertaken in LEA-secured adult learning; and
- the processes affecting wider outcomes such as health benefits and active citizenship – whether these merely correlate with learning or are causally related.

The priority now is to develop more longitudinal work to shed light on these issues. DfES has plans in place for such research, with samples drawn both from the general population and from participants in specific programmes such as adult and community learning. Work is already under way on the long-term impact of information, advice and guidance. These studies will build on previous research such as *Pathways in Adult Learning* (Finch and La Valle, 1999) which tracked the progress of learners and non-learners from 1997 to 1999. Figure 3 shows the powerful impact of employment-related motivation on participation in learning.

Figure 3: Progression of NALS 97 non-learners: vocational/non-vocational

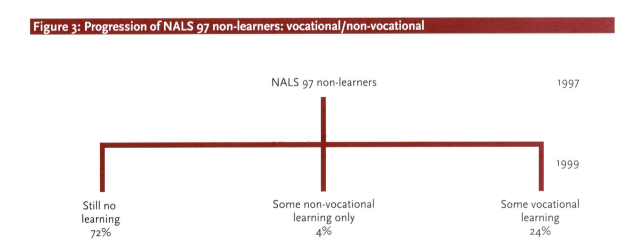

Source: Finch, S. and La Valle, I. (1999). Base: all NALS 97 non-learners

Applying research findings to policy

Research helps us to understand the detailed anatomy of issues, and to identify priorities for action. In 2001 a quarter of adults, looking back at the previous three years of their lives, said that they had done no learning (Blake and La Valle 2001). Among these, more than two in five said that they would have liked to – but could not, for a variety of reasons. These included nervousness about going back into a classroom (reported by 26% of "non-learners"), difficulty paying course fees (27%), lack of time due to family (30%), or simply not knowing about learning opportunities locally (28%). Forty-five per cent of non-learners would have liked to have done some learning. The main factors that would have facilitated their learning were funding (25 per cent), advice (19 per cent) and improved job chances (17 per cent).

Clearly such findings, and those from the NIACE surveys, are highly relevant to the design of policy to bring more people into learning. During the University for Industry's inception, we re-analysed our existing data to inform Ufi's targeting and marketing. This analysis looked at how far the reported learning had been self-initiated. It split the survey population into "self-starters", "yes-buts" and "resisters". Our analyses have informed discussions with Treasury on policy concerning target groups for adult learning policy – looking at past learning (including who paid fees) and anticipated future learning. Findings on the local availability of learning opportunities informed policy development on Lifelong Learning Partnerships and on support for LEAs to develop their Lifelong Learning strategies. The Office for National Statistics has used our information in publications including *Social Focus on Women and Men* and *Social Focus on Older People*. The research underpinned the baseline and achievement measures for the Government's National Learning Target for participation in adult learning, which fell due in 2002 and was met. At the time of writing (2002), NALS findings are being used extensively in a review of the funding of adult learning.

The NALS definition of learning has been incorporated into the Labour Force Survey. This allows us to draw on a much larger sample, and estimate participation by Local Education Authority area and by Learning and Skills Council local office area. This will enable better tracking of groups who are local priorities for widening participation. The latest NALS and LFS estimates for adult participation in learning are the same, at 76% (ONS 2002b; Fitzgerald, Taylor and La Valle 2003, forthcoming). Question coverage in the LFS is inevitably less detailed than in NALS because the LFS has a much wider remit. However, the LFS yields a reliable time series and has a big sample that can be split many ways.

Analysing policies aimed at increasing and widening participation

As well as researching levels of participation, DfES research looks at what affects those levels and what might help to raise them, keeping in close touch with the policy context. The first report of the National Advisory Group for Continuing Education and Lifelong Learning, NAGCELL

(Fryer 1997) said that more emphasis should be placed on the home, the community and the workplace, as places of learning. The Government recognised (Department for Education and Employment 1998) the importance of learning as an end in itself and in supporting social inclusion, civic and public life and personal and spiritual fulfilment. DfES is closely examining these rationales, for example through the work of the Centre for Research on the Wider Benefits of Learning, reported elsewhere in this volume. The White Paper *Learning to Succeed* (Department for Education and Employment 1999) – the precursor of the Learning and Skills Act 2000 – set out how the Government is working to extend and improve the demand for and supply of learning opportunities in order to ensure that everyone has access to high quality, relevant learning at times, locations and places that suit them. The White Paper noted that many adults are looking to learn in informal, self-directed and flexible ways.

Community-based learning has an important role here. A literature review (Callaghan *et al.* 2001) finds great variation in participation between LEA areas, but a consensus that best practice involves an approach that engages creatively with groups and individuals and meets them on their own terms and their own territory; involves the voluntary and community sectors in staff development; focuses efforts to improve the retention of learners on the early stages of the learning experience; helps individuals to make progress, taking a well-structured but gradual approach to involving learners where appropriate in further, more formal provision; and uses accreditation where it motivates rather than deters the learner.

An evaluation of the Adult and Community Learning Fund (Field *et al.* 2001) reports on "what works" in engaging new learners:

- Direct person-to-person recruitment, drawing on existing contacts
- Inspiration and example, encouraging diffident learners to continue
- Building the curriculum on the basis of needs identified by learners and potential learners themselves
- Flexible teaching, combining serious learning with fun
- "Learning by stealth", so that learning is a natural extension of other activities such as a hobby or voluntary commitment
- Building group cohesion and mutual peer group support as a way of shoring up fragile learning identity and maximising retention

Information and communication technologies (ICT) have an important role in learning today. There is a clear correlation between lack of ICT access and socio-economic disadvantage. This has been described as a "Digital Divide", parallel to the "Learning Divide". ICT is becoming important both for individuals' search for appropriate learning opportunities, and for actual learning online. Of those with access to the internet, 44 per cent had used it to get information about learning. Among parents with internet access, over half (55 per cent) had used it to help with their children's learning. (Blake and La Valle).

Access to the basic technology remains unequal, however. Eighty per cent of households in the highest gross income decile have internet access, compared to only 11% in the lowest decile, and 40% for all households (ONS 2002). Cost incentives are still the most likely to be cited to encourage those in disadvantaged groups and areas to use computers and the Internet in future (Taylor Nelson Sofres 2002).

Evaluation of a pilot programme to tackle the Digital Divide (Hall Aitken Associates 2002a) found that around half of those re-interviewed twelve months after their initial involvement indicated that attending the centres had definitely helped them secure a job, secure a better job or move on to further education or training. A first report (Hall Aitken Associates 2002b) on the full roll-out of this programme (UK online centres supported by the Capital Modernisation Fund) found that about three in five of centre users were from priority socio-economic target groups but that the level of home *access* to ICT among users was not greatly below the national average, suggesting a degree of policy deadweight. However, the evidence gave strong support to the original policy rationale in that users first came to the centres with low levels of ICT *skill*, and thus with a clear need for learning.

It is important that people take part in learning provision that is specifically appropriate for them. Information, advice and guidance services are important here. A recent study of guidance for employed people (Killeen 2000) showed that:

- 80% of users found the services helpful;
- the guidance sample were more than twice as likely to get a qualification from a course they had initiated than the comparison sample; but
- overall there was no indication that the guidance group improved earnings more than the comparison group, except through increased hours working – which the guidance sample were twice as likely to have.

In conclusion

"How many adult learners are there?" A simple question – but there is no simple answer unless it is clear what you mean by 'learners', what you mean by 'adult', and what you mean by 'how many'. Further, there is a story to tell about who takes part in the various kinds of learning and who does not, and why. These issues are at the centre of policymaking on adult learning, and therefore at the heart of the Government's efforts to build an evidence base to support the development of policy.

References

ACACE (1982) *Adults: their educational experience and needs* Leicester, Advisory Council for Adult and Continuing Education

Aldridge F. and Sargant N. (2002) *Adult learning and social division: a persistent pattern: Volume 1* Leicester, NIACE

Beinart, S. and Smith, P. (1998) *National Adult Learning Survey 1997,* Sheffield, Department for Education and Employment Research Report 49

Blake, M. and La Valle, I. (2001) *National Adult Learning Survey 2001* Sheffield, Department for Education and Skills Research Brief 321 / Research Report 321
http://www.dfes.gov.uk/research/data/uploadfiles/RB321.doc
http://www.dfes.gov.uk/research/data/uploadfiles/RR321.doc

Callaghan, G. *et al.* (2001) *Who? Why? What? Where? A literature review on adult and community learning* Sheffield, Department for Education and Skills
http://www.dfes.gov.uk/research/data/uploadfiles/RB262.doc
http://www.dfes.gov.uk/research/data/uploadfiles/RR262.doc

Department for Education and Employment (1998) *The Learning Age: a renaissance for a new Britain,* London, The Stationery Office

Department for Education and Employment (1999) *Learning to Succeed: a new framework for post-16 learning*, London, The Stationery Office

Field, J. *et al.* (2001) *An Evaluation of the Adult and Community Learning Fund* Sheffield, Department for Education and Skills
http://www.dfes.gov.uk/research/data/uploadfiles/RB284.doc
http://www.dfes.gov.uk/research/data/uploadfiles/RR284.doc

Finch, S. and La Valle, I. (1999) *Pathways in Adult Learning* Sheffield, Department for Education and Employment

Fitzgerald R., La Valle I. and Taylor R. (2003, forthcoming) *National Adult Learning Survey (NALS) 2002* Sheffield, Department for Education and Skills

Fryer, R.H. (1997) *Learning for the Twenty-First Century, First Report of National Advisory Group for Continuing Education and Lifelong Learning* London, NAGCELL

Hall Aitken Associates (2002a) *Evaluation of Pioneer and Pathfinder UK online centres: follow-up*

study Sheffield, Department for Education and Skills
http://www.dfes.gov.uk/research/data/uploadfiles/RB362.doc
http://www.dfes.gov.uk/research/data/uploadfiles/RR362.doc

Hall Aitken Associates (2002b) *Evaluation of CMF-funded UK online centres* Sheffield, Department for Education and Skills
http://www.dfes.gov.uk/research/data/uploadfiles/RB368.doc
http://www.dfes.gov.uk/research/data/uploadfiles/RR368.doc

Killeen, J. and White, M. (2000) *The impact of careers guidance on adult employed people* London, Department for Education and Employment Research Report 226
http://www.dfes.gov.uk/research/data/uploadfiles/RB226.doc
http://www.dfes.gov.uk/research/data/uploadfiles/RR226.doc

NIAE (1970) *Adult Education – Adequacy of Provision*, National Institute of Adult Education

ONS (2002a) *Internet Access: First Release July 2002* London, Office for National Statistics

ONS (2002b) *Annual Local Area Labour Force Survey*, London, Office for National Statistics
http://www.statistics.gov.uk/llfs

Sargant, N. (1991) *Learning and "leisure"* Leicester, NIACE

Sargant, N. *et al.* (1997) *The Learning Divide* Leicester, NIACE

Sargant, N. (2000) *The Learning Divide Revisited* Leicester, NIACE

Taylor Nelson Sofres (2002) *Trends in ICT Access and Use* Sheffield, Department for Education and Skills
http://www.dfes.gov.uk/research/data/uploadfiles/RB358.doc
http://www.dfes.gov.uk/research/data/uploadfiles/RR358.doc

CHAPTER THREE

The benefits of learning

Professor Tom Schuller, Dean of the Faculty of Continuing Education at Birkbeck College
and Co-director of the Wider Benefits of Learning Research Centre

Introduction

NIACE's surveys give us an invaluable picture of trends in adult participation in learning. Other contributions to this volume analyse these trends, taking advantage of the build up of data over time. The survey is generally referred to as the 'participation survey', accurately reflecting the fact that it has always concentrated on whether or not people take part in learning. This basic issue is then examined in terms of a host of variables in order to reveal the differential patterns of participation, across class, gender, geographical location and so on.

Such a focus on participation is not surprising. But the 2002 survey includes for the first time information on the benefits or changes which people report from their learning. That is the subject of this chapter, which has three parts. First I consider some reasons why the focus has been so much on whether or not people take part, and so little on what happens as a result. Secondly, I report on work carried out with colleagues at the Centre for Research on Wider Benefits of Learning. Thirdly, I present findings from the 2002 survey which relate to the benefits issue.

The WBL Centre was set up by the DfES in 1999 with the following brief:

i)   to produce and apply methods for measuring and analysing the contribution that learning makes to wider goals including (but not limited to) social cohesion, active citizenship, active ageing and improved health;

ii)   to devise and apply improved methods for measuring the value and contribution of forms of learning including (but not limited to) community based adult learning where the outcomes are not necessarily standard ones such as qualifications;

iii) to develop an overall framework to evaluate the impact of the lifelong learning strategy being put in place to 2002 and beyond to realise the vision set out in the former DfEE's Green Paper 'the Learning Age' (CM 3790) February 1998, covering both economic and non-economic outcomes.

The Centre's first phase involved preliminary scoping work and literature reviews covering these broad fields (Schuller *et al* 2001; Plewis and Preston 2001), together with associated analyses of particular aspects (Bynner 2000, Bynner and Egerton 2001, Preston & Hammond 2002). The second phase comprised the fieldwork briefly reported below, and linked work on large-scale datasets (Feinstein 2002, Blackwell and Bynner 2002).

Ignoring the outcome end

One of our first tasks in the WBL Centre, naturally, was to review the work that had already been done in the area. It was striking how little attention has historically been paid to what actually happens as a result of people taking part in learning, compared with the huge amount of analysis devoted to motivation and participation. Moreover my own experience has been that discussions of outcomes or effects have an innate tendency to revert to issues of participation and the barriers to it. The natural assumption is that the outcomes of participation are positive and more or less self-evident. (This is, incidentally, true in relation to work-related training as well as other forms of education, which is all the more surprising given that the former can be assumed to reflect more hard-headed economic decision-making, which should presumably be accompanied by equally hard-headed assessment of results.) It seems hard for people generally to sustain a focus on the outcome end, and it is worth reflecting on why this is. There are both political and pragmatic reasons.

Those responsible for policy naturally tend to concentrate on participation rates because these have an immediate salience. Their apparent significance can be quickly grasped, and a message deduced and broadcast. Targets can be set. This is not cynical comment, but a reflection of political life. But adult educators also tend to take it for granted that participation is what counts, since adult education is to self-evidently a good thing. Their livelihoods, or at least their standing and morale, depend on buoyant demand. So practitioners are keen to maintain a focus on participation without necessarily examining any of the underlying assumptions.

Pragmatically, estimating and analysing participation is far easier than assessing the effects of learning. Its meaning is generally (though not always) clear. More importantly, the core data is routinely collected, at least for the more formal types of participation. Institutions collect enrolment figures, and reporting of them is now fairly routine, if burdensome.

Finally, researchers who wish to go into greater depth have easier access to current than to past students. Tracing the latter is difficult and expensive. There is therefore a natural tendency to collect information on people who are studying now, rather than on those who took part some time ago. Current students can of course report on benefits or effects which have already occurred, but can only predict what further effects might ensue.

None of this is to devalue the work done on participation. Nor is it to ignore individual studies done of groups of students, such as female returners. It is merely a reminder of the way our understanding is weighted towards the input rather than the outcome end of the process.

Some findings from WBL fieldwork

This section summarises results from the first major piece of fieldwork conducted by the Centre (for a fuller account see Schuller *et al* 2002). It comprised 140 biographical interviews with individuals aged over 16, in three different locations. Our conceptual framework took the form of a triangle, with human capital, social capital and personal identity at the three corners; inside this we located the various outcome categories in which we were interested: health, family life, civic participation and so on.

One important general finding was the way learning serves to *sustain* as well as to *transform* people's quality of life. We applied this to benefits ranging from individual to collective, as shown in the matrix below:

Figure 1: Learning by age – NALS 2001

Individual

A   B

Personal change   Self-maintenance

Transforming   **Sustaining**

C   D

Community activism   Social fabric

Adaptation and change

One of our projects focussed on how learning helped parents with young children to manage the changes brought about by parenthood. A major benefit, especially to mothers, is that education provided them with a change of scene, routine and company. It enables, or pushes, them to get away from the home and their children for a while, and to maintain or recover their sense of identity as an adult. The strength of the effect ranges from mild to a sense that their participation saved them from severe mental health problems.

Education gives a structure to people's lives. This may be on a daily/weekly basis, where otherwise they felt they were losing control; or in the sense of giving them a focus and goal, long- or short-term, such that they could see a way to progress beyond the current phase of their lives.

Education provides the confidence, skills and opportunity to access knowledge relevant to new situations occasioned by parenting. This is obvious where it refers to parenting courses or other similar learning. But education also enables people to draw on knowledge sources, notably books; and gives them the opportunity to do so by furnishing access to libraries.

English language training is crucial to parents who do not speak English, so they can understand the educational and health needs of their children and access the appropriate services.

Overall, learning of all kinds enables parents to retain their sense of being part of a wider, adult society, to contribute to it and to access support from it.

Family lives

There are a number of ways in which family members participating in learning benefits the rest of the family. Taking part themselves in learning strengthens the general value parents place on their own children's learning. Parents come to understand more of specific aspects of their children's schooling, for example the curriculum in maths, English or computing/IT, and can offer direct support.

Parents may learn skills directly enabling them to improve their parenting, for example in devising games with their children or understanding their developmental patterns better, and managing their behaviour more effectively. They also develop better communication skills generally.

Learning may improve relationships between partners, or between adults and their parents or the wider family. This may be by providing common subjects of interest around which communication can improve; but more generally it is likely to be because of enhanced respect and self-confidence.

There can be negative or double-edged effects. For example, a mother's participation in education will reduce the time and energy she has available for her family, or her raised aspirations will cause her to give up serving other members of the family.

Health

We found little evidence of education directly improving physical health. The exceptions were some older people. However mental health effects of various kinds were very clear.

Education can help directly as a therapeutic activity for people with mental health problems. More commonly reported was the preventative effect, where respondents talked about how education had helped them avoid, minimise or address depression. Much of it relates to benefits which stop short of the medical, but which have significant implications for the interrelationships between education, health and community policies.

Learning helps people communicate more effectively with professionals, either directly by understanding the language or indirectly by having the confidence to express themselves and ask questions. It widens access to written information on health issues. In addition, classes provide a forum for the formal and informal exchange of health-related information.

Education can increase self-awareness and self-understanding. In general the effect is positive, enhancing people's sense of autonomy and efficacy, with further positive consequences. But it can be risky for the individual and their family, putting in question fundamental issues of personal identity.

Social capital and social cohesion

There are various mechanisms through which tolerance and positive learning about social values takes place: social mix (the sheer fact of meeting people from other social groups and backgrounds); role models provided by teachers and other students; and subject content, providing better understanding.

Participation in education also provides the physical opportunities through which people can put their civic skills to use. This may be related to the school or college, or to wider community issues.

A further benefit is a strengthening of social networks. We identified three ways in which this occurs: individuals' entry into new networks; the extension of existing networks; and the restoration of networks which had in some way lapsed or declined.

We found striking examples of civic activity relating to particular lifecycle stages. In addition to the targeted population of parents of young children, older people's contribution to such activity is strongly aided by learning. The gendering of civic activity reinforces the need to recognise informal as well as formal types.

NIACE survey: benefits and changes

The 2002 NIACE survey includes welcome evidence on benefits and changes which respondents were able to identify as a consequence of their learning. Respondents were given a list of 15 possible effects stemming from their learning. These ranged from job-related aspects (promotion, earnings, job satisfaction) through issues of personal wellbeing (health, self-confidence) to social connections and involvement. This analysis reports only on simple cross-tabulations; it cannot give us any depth, but is enough to illuminate some of the picture.

One rather sobering result is that 1 in 7 of the respondents reported no changes as a result of their learning (or at least none from the list presented). This may mean that the learning had been ineffectual, with no subsequent effect; or that they had simply enjoyed it as consumption; or possibly that they set a rigorous level of causality, and were unwilling to attribute benefits directly to the learning. The 'none' response was highest, at 20% plus, amongst the unemployed and those with least access to modern communication technology, which suggests that there are structural reasons why people do not perceive themselves to have benefited.

I turn now to evidence broadly relating to the areas covered in the WBL fieldwork reported above:

Adaptation/resilience

The most commonly reported benefit was an improvement in self-confidence and a feeling of personal development, with 29% of the sample listing these. 'Self-confidence' is surely the most commonly reported benefit in the literature generally. Yet we can ask what this newly-found confidence leads to. Greater individual psychological security, more competent handling of relationships in the home, more effective performance at work, and so on – arguably this effect is fundamental, but it needs unpacking and differentiation. This is where detailed qualitative work can be crucial in illuminating the paths by which changes translate into actual benefits. There is also an interesting debate to be had over whether people's self-confidence can be excessively enhanced, to their own or others' detriment.

34% of those in social class DE reported enhanced confidence, compared to 24% of ABs. People who have not been successful at school are more likely to suffer low self-confidence, especially in relation to education. So the mere fact of participating with a modicum of success can have an enormous effect. But the fact that nearly 1 in 4 from the top socio-economic range also report this shows that there is continuing work to be done at all levels. The highest proportion reporting change under this heading was 43%, by fulltime students.

Family life

A tiny proportion reported a positive effect on family life – 4% of the total, rising to 7% of those with children aged 5-15. However the question did refer only to whether their children or family had become more interested in learning, rather than about broader positive effects of the kind we noted above.

Health

Only 4% reported an improvement in health. This is on the face of it surprising. There is a strong correlation between health and educational levels (Hammond 2002), and much anecdotal and qualitative evidence of people feeling better as a result of participation. There is however a particular angle to this. Our WBL work suggests that it is more in the sphere of mental than physical health that benefits are to be expected. Survey evidence is more likely to refer to physical health, because this is the more conventional interpretation and because of the persistent stigma attached to mental health.

Health – especially mental or psychological health – is also an interesting illustration of one measurement problem. It is easier to measure discrete and visible or tangible change, such as the gaining of a qualification or an increase in earnings. Whilst some health changes can fall into that category, they may lie more under the surface. As depicted in Figure 1 above we suggested thinking of changes (in all domains) as running along a spectrum from the 'transformative' to the 'sustaining'. Much of the health-related effects may be in sustaining people's mental and physical health, preventing decline more than transforming them from 'sick' to 'healthy'.

Social participation

Second only to self-confidence was the making of friends, with 26% reporting this. We need to distinguish here between expectations and actual outcomes: 32% of those currently studying responded under this heading, but only 19% of those who had finished, which suggests some predictable drop off after the course finishes. The figure was highest among young people, peaking in the 20-24 age group dipping in middle age but rising again for those over 55. We would expect this from the lifecycle squeeze, with the middle age groups preoccupied by family and career.

Making friends is part of developing social networks. The highest proportion of all was reported by fulltime students, at 52%. The importance of this has been demonstrated by some excellent work by Nick Emler, who studied five different groups of young people, from unemployed to fulltime university students, and showed how powerful education is as an enabler of network-building. We need to reflect on the relationship between the intrinsic value of making more friends and the additional, and often powerful, instrumental value of network membership.

The link between education and civic participation does not get much support, though the question was limited to whether or not they got more involved in local events. Only 5% reported yes, with just a single unemployed person (out of 86) in this category); on the other hand 11% of the retired did say they had become more involved, which is a reasonably healthy contribution to civic engagement in the third age.

To conclude this section, I report on a few other general findings:

- 21% reported getting or expecting a qualification as a benefit or change. It could of course signal a change in status – possession of qualification – without this impacting at all on the person's life. We need to think through the distinction between intermediate and final outcomes, even though this can turn into a game of Russian dolls. Acquiring a qualification is a clear enough benefit, but is hardly an intrinsic benefit, except for those who enjoy having their walls papered with certificates. On the other hand, the mere possession of a qualification can do wonders for people's self-esteem, whether or not it serves any other instrumental purpose. So already we are in a complex web of interacting factors.

- 15% said that their work had or might become more satisfying. The highest level of reporting here was from the 45-54 year olds. This goes along with their rather lower expectations about increased earnings, and suggests that people who are past the mid-point in their working lives may be more interested in intrinsic rather than extrinsic rewards from work. This poses an interesting challenge to conventional human capital theory, where investment in learning should be reflected in earnings. Even where it is not, it may nevertheless result in enhanced productivity, since this tends to be linked to job satisfaction.

- The rural/urban divide is one of the most ignored in educational research, and arguably more broadly. In part this is because of the difficulty of establishing boundaries between the two, and the need to distinguish between different forms of rurality (see Clarke *et al* 2002). Nevertheless, it is worth reporting that on every single dimension rural inhabitants report lower levels of benefit or change than their urban counterparts. In most cases the difference is small, and certainly not statistically significant. But noticeably few of the rural respondents (3%, compared with 7% of urbans) expected to move on to further study; fewer had got or expected to get qualifications or make new friends. Some of this general difference may be mediated by social deprivation, given the generally lower standards of living enjoyed by rural dwellers, but it raises significant questions about how to build into policy consideration of this dimension.

- There were lower levels of benefit/change reported in Scotland than elsewhere on every single aspect except for being helped in the current job. This reminds me of work John Field and I carried out a few years ago, to explain apparently lower levels of participation in adult education in Scotland and Northern Ireland compared with England. In Scotland it turned out that much of this could be explained by reference to the interpretation of the question: Scots set a higher threshold in their understanding of what constituted participation, so that very brief episodes did not count for them. Possibly they set higher standards also for significance of effect, and reported fewer benefits because they do not think minor changes are worth reporting.

Concluding note: the challenge of causality

I began by noting the reluctance of many people to focus on outcomes rather than participation. I conclude by noting the real difficulty of tracing causal relations. This is not just a technical difficulty. One of the most surprising things I have learnt in my WBL work, as it seeks to integrate different modes of research and analysis, is the divergence of understanding which exists in relation to cause. If we are to understand how adult education actually affects people, materially and subjectively, we need to be clear about this, without spending all our time in methodological or semantic debate. The NIACE surveys do not solve this particular problem, but they do give us very helpful benchmarks to measure change.

References

Blackwell, L. & Bynner, J. (2002) *Learning, Family Formation and Dissolution*, London, Centre for Research on the Wider Benefits of Learning (in press).

Bynner, J. & Egerton, M. (2001) *The Wider Benefits of Higher Education*, Bristol, Higher Education Funding Council for England.

Clarke, R. *et al* (2002) Lifelong *Learning in Rural Areas: A Report to the Countryside Agency*, Birkbeck/NIACE

Feinstein, L. (2002a) *Quantitative Estimates of the Social Benefits of Learning, 1: Crime*, London, Centre for Research on the Wider Benefits of Learning (in press).

Feinstein, L. (2002b) *Quantitative Estimates of the Social Benefits of Learning, 2: Health*, London, Centre for Research on the Wider Benefits of Learning (in press).

Hammond, C. (2002) *Learning to be healthy*, Report 5, Wider Benefits of Learning Centre, London, Institute of Education

Plewis I. & Preston J., (2001) *Evaluating the Benefits of Lifelong Learning*, Centre for Research on the Wider Benefits of Learning, London, Institute of Education/Birkbeck College

Schuller, T. *et al*, (2001) *Modelling and Measuring the Wider Benefits of Learning: A Synthesis* Centre for Research on the Wider Benefits of Learning, London, Institute of Education/Birkbeck College

Schuller, T, Brassett-Grundy, A., Green, A. Hammond, C. and Preston,J. (2002) *Learning, Continuity and Adult Life*, Centre for Research in the Wider Benefits of Learning Report 3, London, Institute of Education

Social capital and lifelong learning: survey findings on the relationship between sociability and participation

Professor John Field, Director of Academic Innovation and
Continuing Education, University of Stirling

People who are sociable are more likely to be doing some learning. People who are involved in their community are more likely to be adult learners than those who are less involved. People who go out frequently for their leisure are also more likely to participate in learning. Conversely, though, people whose leisure interests revolve around their home are, on the whole, less likely to be adult learners. These findings emerge from the 2002 adult learning survey, and they should be of considerable value to anyone interested in adult learning. They are also relevant to the continuing discussion over community and participation in what has steadily become a highly individualised society.

This discussion has particularly crystallised around the concept of social capital, which is now often associated with the work of the American political scientist Robert Putnam (Putnam 2000; see also Field 2003). The core idea of social capital is the suggestion that people's connections have value. They allow people to co-operate for mutual benefit, and gain access to resources that they can then use. A preliminary study suggested that this general insight could be applied to the understanding of patterns of participation in learning (Schuller and Field 1998). The survey data allow for a more systematic and evidence based review of this proposition.

People's learning always takes place in a wider social context. Until recently, though, relatively little was known about how that social context was related to the learning that people do in adult life. In particular, there have been few attempts to examine the relationship between adult learning and what we might call the meso-level of people's institutional affiliations and their involvement in a range of associations from the family to civic movements of various kinds. At the macro-level, research into the social context of participation has been limited to a broad recognition that such general social factors as socio-economic status, ethnicity and gender appear to play a powerful role in determining people's opportunities and shaping their decisions (e.g. Sargant 1997). If large-scale surveys tell us about the wider statistical trends, studies influenced by situated learning and experiential learning have tended to emphasise the immediate environment of the learning situation (Lave and Wenger, 1991), while life history researchers generally explore the subjective experiences and perceptions of individuals (Merrill 1999; West 1996). While these studies have shed a great deal of light on what we might call the macro and micro levels of adult learning, they have generally failed to acknowledge the patterns of social interaction and association within which individuals' immediate learning environments are embedded.

The 2002 adult learning survey included a number of questions which should allow us to explore this meso level of social association more closely, and see whether it has any wider implications for people's participation in adult learning. Of course, this is far from being completely virgin territory (Jarvis 1987). In more recent years, a number of researchers have noted that people who are active citizens also tend to be lifelong learners (Benn 2000; Field 1991). Arguably, most European popular education movements were based on the premise that civic engagement and adult learning were closely related. Similarly, there is some evidence that those who take part in various cultural activities are more likely to take part in learning (Sargant 1997). An analysis of the International Adult Literacy Survey shows that countries which scored high in respect of adult education participation also tended to score highly on participation in voluntary associations, and generally showed higher levels of trust in other people (Tuijnman and Boudard 2001, 40). Family connections have also been shown to have a very powerful influence on people's participation in learning, with an impact that apparently stretches back for at least three generations (Gorard and Rees, 2002). So there appears to be something of an emerging pattern which suggests that people's connections are somehow tied to their learning, in ways that could have considerable practical significance.

The 2002 survey contained a number of questions that were designed to shed light on the relationship between social capital and adult learning. These questions can be grouped into three broad areas. First, it included questions about people's main leisure interests, which covered a number of activities that were likely to involve associations with other people (including voluntary service, attendance at a place of worship, participation in sporting activity, and socialising with others), as well as activities that focussed more on the home (such as gardening). Second, it asked about frequency of engagement in a number of activities, some of which were associated with higher levels of interaction with others (including attendance at cinemas, community centres, and places of worship). Third, it posed a question about people's general levels of trust. This question was taken from the World Values Survey, and while it only offers a very crude indicator of trust, the responses might indicate whether this dimension of social capital is worth further study. This chapter draws on the responses to all three sets of questions.

This chapter addresses two key questions. First, what does the survey tell us about the relationship between people's engagement in a variety of social connections and their engagement with learning? Second, does it suggest any consequences for those who work with adult learners? To summarise briefly, the survey confirms that there is a very strong link between connectedness and learning: those who engage most in socialising are more likely than average to be learners. There are some exceptions, and these too are instructive, and indeed point to possible explanations. Nevertheless, although the survey is very suggestive as to the causes of this link, it offers a basis less for confident conclusions than for reasonably well-informed speculation. This may in turn indicate where further research, qualitative as well as quantitative, might prove helpful.

Social engagement and adult learning

The first question to consider is whether people who are more connected with others are more or less likely to be adult learners. One possibility is that adult learning is not going to attract people who have a wide range of social connections. Firstly, it is possible that the two are in competition with one another for people's time and resources: after all, people have a limited amount of money and time to spend, and they might decide that they can either learn something, or they can socialise, but they cannot afford to do both. Secondly, it is possible that social connections can deliver many of the same benefits as learning (such as access to a new job); indeed, by providing opportunities for informal learning, they can even deliver access to new skills and information (Field and Spence, 2000). So it is possible that the two are competing with, rather than complementing each other. Yet the survey results tend to support an alternative hypothesis: namely, that social capital and lifelong learning are largely complementary.

In analysing the responses, I have divided people's leisure interests into those that are largely home based and those involving a high level of interaction with others. Those which intrinsically require people to interact with others were attending a place of worship, taking part in social activities (family, friends, disco, eating out, pub, etc), participating in sports (including keep-fit and walking), performing music, and lastly volunteering and committee work. Do-it-yourself (in this survey including handicrafts), indoor games, knitting and sewing, and gardening were all defined as typically home-based activities for the purposes of this analysis. In all those interests involving a high level of interaction with others, the survey found that participants were more likely than the population at large to be adult learners. Levels of current and recent learning were above the national average for people involved in attending a place of worship, taking part in social activities (family, friends, disco, eating out, pub, etc), participating in sports (including keep-fit and walking), volunteering and committee work, and musical performance. In the case of musical performance, 66.5% of participants said that they were current and recent learners, as against 42.3% of all adults responding; 62.6% of committee members/volunteers were recent learners. In each case, those involved in high levels of interaction were also less likely to describe themselves as never having done any learning than were the general population.

In all cases, all but one of these groups score above the average when it comes to future learning; in particular, 62.6% of the musical performers and 51.0% of the committee members/volunteers expected to do some learning in the future, as against 40.6% of the general population. The exception to this pattern is the group who expressed an interest in worship, who is no more or less likely than the population at large to expect to learn in the future.

The picture is somewhat more complex when it comes to home-based interests. In two cases, participants were more likely than average to be learners: 49.7% of people interested in under-taking D-I-Y/handicrafts are current/recent learners, and 56.9% of people interested in indoor games are current/recent learners, well above the national average of 42.3%. In the case of people playing indoor games, it could be argued that theirs is an activity that is home based, but not isolated. Most indoor games require a partner, and sometimes several, so the finding here is consistent with the general association between connectedness and adult learning. In the other two cases – knitting/sewing and gardening – people are less likely to report current/recent learning. Among keen gardeners, only 38.3% are current learners, and among sewers, knitters and embroiderers the figure reaches 36.3%. Both of these latter two groups are also above average in the proportion reporting that they have never undertaken any learning, and below average in the proportion expecting to do any learning. Both of these interests are not only based in the home, but they do not require any interaction with others, and can be undertaken in isolation (it is sometimes said that people prefer to spend time in their garden for precisely this reason).

So far, the survey has shown that people who are interested in activities that involve socialising with others are more likely to be learners. They are also more likely to have plans for learning in the future. Conversely, it has also shown that people who are interested in more solitary home based pursuits are generally less likely to be learners, and they are less likely to plan to learn something in the future. These findings are broadly consistent with the general hypothesis of a positive association between social capital and participation in adult learning.

Leisure commitments and adult learning

The chapter now considers the relationship between frequency of people's involvement and their participation in learning. Whereas the previous set of questions asked people what their main interests were, this set of questions was concerned with how often people did things. While some of these activities directly complement learning (such as visiting a library), others are likely to compete with it (such as visiting the cinema). Thus the results to these questions are important, since frequent participation in an activity must consume time and resources that cannot then be used for other activities, including learning. Yet the findings suggest that going out and learning do not compete but on the contrary are strongly associated with one another.

Broadly, this part of the survey shows that people who are currently studying are much more likely to go out for leisure purposes than people who are not studying. As might be expected, the association is very strong in respect of activities that tend to go together with learning. One in five of current learners claims to visit a public library once a week, against less than one in ten of those whose learning was over three years ago, or who have done no learning since leaving school. They were three times as likely to report visiting museums at least once a month, and four times as likely to visit an art gallery. Surprisingly, though, current learners were also much more likely to visit the cinema regularly (8% did so at least once a week, compared with 2% of non-learners). Current learners were twice as likely to visit the theatre at least once a month, and three times as likely to attend concerts. They were also more likely to visit community centres and social clubs (15% of current learners do so once a week, as against 12% of non-learners) and places of worship (18% of current learners, 12% of non-learners do so once a week).

This pattern is also reflected in people's plans for future learning. Again, this is not confined to the predictable patterns, which we might expect to find among those who frequently visit libraries, museums and art galleries. All of these groups are much more likely than other people to expect to learn. Just to take one example, a clear majority of frequent library-users (that is, those who go at least once a week) expect to learn in the future, while almost two thirds of those who rarely or never visit libraries do not expect to learn. Yet the same is broadly true of other people who go out a lot. In the case of cinemagoers, the association with future learning is even stronger than among library users. Once more, almost two thirds of those who rarely or never use cinemas do not expect to learn; among those who go at least weekly, though, 71% expect to learn in the future. This pattern is also found for theatregoers and concertgoers; while less marked among those who frequently attend community centres/social clubs and places of worship, the survey still shows that they are more likely to expect to learn than average.

Finally, there is some evidence in the survey that the most outgoing people tend to do different kinds of learning from those who go out less often. Among learners who are also frequent cinema goers, for example, the most common reasons for study are personal development and educational progression; they also are more likely to be working for a qualification than not. Those who rarely visit a cinema, by contrast, are much more likely to be studying as a result of somebody else's decisions, or for work reasons; they are less likely to be studying for a qualification. A slightly different pattern emerges among those who visit social clubs/community centres. Once again it is those who go least frequently who are most likely to say their learning was "not my choice" or, to a lesser extent, is related to work, but there is no difference between frequent visitors and others as to whether they study for qualifications. In the case of places of worship, it is learners who visit occasionally (less than once a week to once a month) who are most likely to be studying as a result of somebody else's decisions. The most frequent attendees are more likely to be working for qualifications, while those who rarely or never attend are more likely not to be aiming for qualifications. These findings suggest a degree of complexity in the peoples' learning careers, in which lifestyle, age and social position intersect with degree of social engagement to produce particular patterns of participation. Yet one consistent pattern appears from the data: those who are engaged in the most active social and cultural lives are also the most likely to be in control of their own learning, and to be doing their learning for educational and personal reasons.

Overall, then, the survey shows no support at all for the common sense view, which suggests that people who spend a lot of time on their leisure interests are unlikely to have spare time to learn. For virtually all areas in the survey, the results show the contrary: those people who visit places like the cinema, clubs, concerts or places of worship more often are the most likely to be learning at present, and are also more likely to expect to learn in future. Of course, as is always the case with statistical evidence about people's behaviour, we should be cautious in interpreting these findings. In particular, the pattern I am describing might be explained by some third factor, particularly age. Young people go out to the cinema more often than older people, and they are also more likely to be studying at college or at work. Without undertaking a more sophisticated analysis of the data, it is still clear that age is responsible for some of the pattern that I have described – but far from all of it. So there is still an association between sociability and participation in learning. People who are adult learners get out a lot more than non learners.

Learning and trust

So far, the survey findings tend to support the view that people who are more engaged with others are more likely to be learners, and also more likely to expect to learn in the future. This suggests a positive correlation between social capital and adult learning. The survey also asked people about their levels of trust. This is often taken as a very approximate indicator of the extent to which people are able to co-operate with each other. While it might be argued that trust is a product of social capital rather than one of its ingredients, what matters for this study is whether there is a positive relationship between people's capacity for co-operation with others on the one hand, and their involvement in learning on the other. The purpose of including a question on this topic was mainly to find out whether there was any basis for thinking that levels trust might be an important influence on adult learning. The findings on this issue are indecisive, and somewhat complex.

In the survey, people were asked how far they agreed or disagreed with the statement: "In general most people can be trusted". This statement comes from the highly respected World Values Survey (WVS), and has been used by Putnam among others as one indicator of social capital. Respondents were asked to choose one of five options, ranging from "Agree strongly" to "Disagree strongly". The largest single group of respondents (49% of the total) opted to "Agree" with the statement; only 7% said they agreed strongly, 19% disagreed and 6% disagreed strongly. A further 18% neither agreed nor disagreed. The survey population as a whole, then, showed a relatively high level of trust, and this held broadly true for non-learners as much as for learners. Taking both current and recent learning together, the following responses were clustered around the mean: those who agreed strongly, those who disagreed, and those who agreed all came in around the average. There were two divergences from this overall pattern: those who neither agreed nor disagreed with the statement were more likely to be learners, and whose who expressed strong disagreement were less likely to be learners. But these were not particularly strong associations. So far, it seems that trust has a limited and slightly complex association with learning; it does not seem to be a significant factor.

It is also difficult to link levels of trust with future learning. People who expect to learn in the future were somewhat more likely to agree with the WVS statement than those who do not expect to learn, as were those who neither agreed nor disagreed. People who agreed strongly were split evenly between those who expect to learn and those who do not; those with the lowest levels of trust were slightly less likely to anticipate future learning, but those who indicated simple disagreement with the WVS statement were slightly more likely to expect to learn.

According to this survey, then, people's levels of trust do not seem to be closely associated with participation in learning. In so far as there is any association, it is a complex one, and not at all straightforward and linear. Admittedly, our question referred only to generalised trust; inquiries into more specific forms of trust might deliver different results. Moreover, trust might be important in respect of some types of learning, but not others. This possibility is confirmed to some extent by the survey, which shows that people with higher levels of trust are well represented among those whose learning is not geared to a qualification. Conversely, people with lower levels of trust are more strongly represented among those learning for a qualification, and less so among those not working towards a qualification. This is consistent with earlier hypotheses based on qualitative data on the importance of trust and networks in fostering informal learning (Field and Spence 2000).

Overall, the survey findings do not provide any evidence that trust is directly connected with participation in learning. This is not to say that there is no connection, but only that this particular way of investigating the relationship proved inconclusive. Further research is needed before coming to any conclusion, however qualified, on this issue. What can be rejected outright is any simple view of the link: there is no evidence here of a straightforward correlation between generalised trust and participation in learning. Yet there is at least a hint, albeit very loose, that generalised trust may be associated with participation in less formal types of learning. Clearly this is an area where further research is likely to prove informative.

Should we ban gardening and encourage adultery?
Implications for policy and practice

In general, the 2002 survey provides compelling evidence of a link between social connectedness and adult learning. Among the findings which are particularly significant in this respect, the survey confirms that the relationship between connectedness and learning holds good for a variety of types of social association, and not only for those which are particularly tied to learning, or have a clearly identified political or campaigning dimension. Some of us will be mightily relieved to discover that adult learning is positively associated with going out to the pub with friends and visiting the cinema, but these activities fall into a wider pattern of engagement, along with such things as becoming active in a voluntary organisation, playing indoor games and taking part in sports. Adult learners are joiners, and vice versa.

One obvious question is whether the converse also follows: in other words, are isolated people less likely to be learners? This is suggested by the example of gardeners, many of whom enjoy their favoured activity in isolation from others. There are also other highly suggestive findings elsewhere in the survey; the questions on life transitions show that some particular circumstances are strongly associated with non-participation in learning, while other changes appear to favour participation. Some of these are obvious and predictable; for example, serious illness is very strongly associated with non-learning, while the loss of a job shows a small association with learning (often, equally predictable, undertaken because of another person's decision). But what is also striking is that retirement and bereavement, both of which remove people from key sources of social support, are associated with much lower levels of participation than average. By contrast, the end of a relationship with a partner is closely and positively associated with much higher levels of participation. It is tempting to speculate on precisely why people who split up with their partner are more likely to learn, but in this context it is probably best left for further investigation.

What practical consequences follow from this clear evidence that connectedness and learning are linked? Before considering this issue, it is important to emphasise the limits to this study. Above all else, this analysis has dealt with relatively simple statistical associations, and these do not help us say which factor is cause and which is effect. We know that social capital often goes hand in hand with participation in learning, but we do not really know how they are linked. It may even be that both are the products of some other factor. For example, we know that both civic engagement and adult learning are linked with other variables such as experience of schooling, socio-economic situation, or generation. Researchers in Germany have also found that people's involvement in learning is bound up with their wider frameworks of values and attitudes (Barz 2000). A more detailed statistical enquiry, possibly involving techniques such as regression analysis, would be required to disentangle the different effects of all of these variables. And only qualitative studies could shed much light on the ways in which people actively integrate episodes of learning into the intricate patterns of their lives. Yet we can set the findings of the 2002 survey alongside other evidence of the importance of connectedness to adult learning, and on this basis we can surely show a reasonably consistent pattern of linkages.

Perhaps the first set of consequences concern the implications for policy. Penalising gardening and promoting adultery is a rather improbable guide to action. Yet if policy makers want to promote adult learning and invest in community building, the evidence of this survey suggests that they should see these goals as closely linked together. Many people may see both adult learning and sociability as desirable in themselves, but the evidence here suggests that these are linked, and even if we do not fully understand the reasons for these linkages, a common set of integrated policy instruments is likely to be mutually reinforcing. Conversely, policy measures which damage learning opportunities will also reduce social interaction; and measures which undermine community will also remove opportunities for learning. Governments across the UK who wish to promote active adult learning may therefore want to increase the active membership of all kinds of associations, and take measures which improve people's leisure opportunities.

Providers also face important messages, including a number relating to the ways in which they set about the marketing of opportunities. First, providers themselves benefit from strong connections. Isolated providers with weak roots in their communities are likely to lose the plot. This is rather different from the current policy messages about partnership, which tend to focus on formal agreements between learning suppliers and other institutions. What I am suggesting is that providers benefit enormously from the social networks – internal and external – of their staff. These networks provide two-way flows of communications, they create reputations and trust, and they facilitate informal co-operation. Providers need to value these connections, and promote them more systematically if they want to grow their own organisational social capital. Moreover, people who construct active social lives will generally be more positively disposed towards learning. Providers therefore benefit from knowing a great deal about the interests and activities of the most active and engaged members of their target communities. They will be able to engage with these active individuals more effectively if their staff includes a lot of people who are known and trusted themselves, either directly or by reputation.

Finally, there is growing recognition of the learning divide and the digital divide; we also need to consider inequalities and disadvantages that arise from isolation. People who are active learners seem to be relatively well integrated into their communities, and they help to make their communities more connected in turn. Those who are not so active as learners tend to be more isolated. While we may not yet know much about causation, one obvious consequence is that policy makers and practitioners may need to consider isolation when targeting resources at need. This is not simply a matter of geographical isolation. Although remote, island and rural communities may well have difficulty in accessing resources, people living in these settings often benefit from strong networks of community support. Isolation may be more common among people in estates where social relationships have broken down than among people whose neighbours, however scattered, are known and trusted. Isolation may also be linked to phases in the life course; we have seen that retirement, bereavement and serious illness are associated with low levels of participation in learning. How can providers connect with people whose social support networks have lost keystones, and help prevent their disconnection becoming permanent?

Of course, survey data at national level can only provide a very partial map of the broad, varied and complex landscape of adult learning. They tell us virtually nothing about the quality of the learning, or of the rich variety of learners' experiences. They are silent on what the learning meant for those who did it. For evidence on these and many other matters, we will need to look elsewhere. Yet the evidence on the link between sociability and learning in the 2002 survey is compelling. While it should certainly serve as the basis for further study, it is sufficiently clear to offer suggestive messages which should guide the development of policy and practice for the future.

References

Barz, H. (2002) *Weiterbildung und soziale Milieus*, Luchterhand Verlag, Neuwied.

Benn, R. (2000) The genesis of active citizenship in the learning society, *Studies in the Education of Adults*, 32, 2, 241-256

Field, J. (1991) Social movements: The cutting edge of European adult education?. *International Journal of University Adult Education*, 30, 1, 1-11.

Field, J. (2003) *Social Capital*, Routledge Falmer, London

Field, J. and Spence, L. (2000) Informal learning and social capital, in F. Coffield (ed.), *The Necessity of Informal Learning*, Policy Press, Bristol, 2000, 32-42

Gorard, S. and Rees, G. (2002) *Creating a Learning Society? Learning careers and policies for lifelong learning*, Policy Press, Bristol

Lave, J. and Wenger, E. (1991) *Situated Learning*, Cambridge, Cambridge University Press

Merrill, B. (1999) *Gender, Change and Identity: mature women students in universities*, Ashgate, Aldershot

Putnam, R. D. (2000) *Bowling Alone: The collapse and revival of American community*, Simon and Schuster, New York

Sargant, N. with J. Field, H. Francis, T. Schuller and A. Tuckett (1997) *The Learning Divide: A report of the findings of a UK-wide survey on adult participation in education and learning*, National Institute of Adult Continuing Education, Leicester

Schuller, T. and Field, J. (1998) Social Capital, Human Capital and the Learning Society, *International Journal of Lifelong Education*, 17, 4, 1998, 226-35

Tuijnman, A. and Boudard, E. (2001) International Adult Literacy Survey: *Adult Education Participation in North America: international perspectives*, Statistics Canada, Ottawa

West, L. (1996) *Beyond Fragments: adults, motivation and higher education – a biographical analysis*, Taylor and Francis, London

Lifelong learning trajectories in Wales: results of the NIACE Adult Learners' Survey 2002

Dr Stephen Gorard, Reader at Cardiff University School of Social Sciences

Abstract

Patterns of lifelong participation in adult education and training in Wales are distinctive within the UK. Participation, qualification, and economic activity tends to be lower than for the other home countries, and remains systematically structured by age, sex and social class. A problem facing practitioners policy-makers attempting to increase participation rates in Wales is the very low population density and accompanying problems of travel to institutions. Wales is therefore a prime site for testing the notion of 'anytime, anyplace' inherent in virtual participation. What this chapter shows is that, so far, technology has simply replicated existing societal divisions. Of a random sample of 1,000 households, no one reported using the University for Industry/learndirect for their most recent learning episode, for example. Perhaps the money spent on initiatives such as these would be better spent on more traditional forms of adult learning, whether involving technology or not.

Introduction

This paper reports some of the findings from the 2002 NIACE Adult Participation in Learning survey in Wales, particularly with respect to patterns of lifelong learning, the determinants of these patterns, and learners' access to technology. The boosted sample of respondents in Wales is around 1,000 for the first time, and allows a more in-depth analysis than previous years. However, it is important to recall that it is not large enough for reliable local disaggregation, nor can it make estimates from previous years any more reliable. The report on the 1996 NIACE survey (Sargant 1997, p. 30) commented that there were marked variations in local patterns of response over time, and to some extent these variations may simply be taken to display the sensitivity of regional analyses to fairly small variations in responses. Therefore, the analysis presented here for Wales has to remain largely a snapshot made possible by the increased sample size for the first time.

Traditionally all measures of educational participation and attainment in Wales have been inferior to those elsewhere in the UK, both at school level and lifelong (Gorard 2000a, 2000b). A variety of national policies have been created to deal with the problem, including provision of learner allowances, targets for participation (Gorard *et al.* 2002), the virtual and satellite college system (Selwyn and Gorard 2002), and individual use of ICT. ICT is seen by many as a technical solution to the barriers of time and space, and travel to and from an institution. The report of the Education and Training Action Group for Wales had this to say:

> Modern information and communications systems, including digital developments, present both opportunities and threats in adult education. ICT can minimise the constraints of time and space: people can learn or gain information about what is available, whenever and wherever they wish – *providing they have access* to modern technology and the confidence to use it (ETAG 1998, p.30, author's emphasis).

The new NIACE survey contains more, and more detailed, questions about individual access to and use of technology for learning. Therefore, perhaps for the first time on a large scale in Wales it is possible to test this notion of overcoming barriers. There is already considerable doubt about the actual role of 'barriers' in preventing access to adult learning opportunities. Evidence is mounting that non-participants in formal educational episodes are not especially deterred by traditional barriers such as time, cost, travel and lack of initial qualification. This evidence comes partly from the role of long-term socio-economic background characteristics, especially the influence of family, in creating a learner identity which does not view current opportunities as appropriate, interesting, or useful (Gorard *et al.* 1999a). Evidence also comes from a model of two separate sets of determinants for extended initial and later learning respectively (Gorard *et al.* 1999b), and from the accounts of widespread informal learning for which barriers are, by their very nature, less relevant (Gorard *et al.* 1999c). Recent NIACE surveys in Wales have confirmed the prediction of Titmus (1994) that there is a substantial sub-set of the population who are 'beyond all attempts to reach them' (see also Harrison 1993, McGivney 1993).

As well as leading to economic competitiveness (perhaps) and social mobility (probably), education is nearly always a genuinely transformative experience for an individual (at least it was in Wales according to Lewis, 1993), and one that impacts on the local community. Learning should not therefore be viewed as an escape route *from* anything, but a normal part of an accomplished life in a democratic society. Viewed in this way, it is not clear that the experiences offered by the virtual college movement, which is of necessity based on a model of information transmission, can be genuinely educational, or that they *can* lead to better reasoning skills, creativity and the ability to value divergent cultures claimed by Roll (1995). Given these severe limitations, it may therefore be seen as completely rational for an individual to decline to participate. Unfortunately, at least partly because progress is measured in terms of the qualification targets used to attract inward investors, such a conclusion is not considered by policy-makers in Wales, where much lifelong learning policy is still prescriptive (Tight 1998).

The analysis is based on the following questions:

- Who among the adult population of Wales are participants in recent learning experiences, and how do they differ from those who are not participants?
- What are the long-term and current determinants of participation in Wales?
- Who among the adult population of Wales have access to various technologies with a capability of delivering learning experiences?
- Does access to technology, particularly ICT, 'create' adult learners and learning experiences?

Method

The 2002 NIACE Adult Participation in Learning survey involved 5,885 households, based on 390 randomised geographical clusters, including a boosted sample of 995 cases from Wales, and re-weighted to reflect appropriate proportions by sex, social class (assessed in terms of AB: professional/managerial, C1: non-manual, C2: manual skilled, and DE: partly- or un-skilled), and standard economic region. The responses have been analysed here in terms of frequencies and cross-tabulations. All figures for Wales are presented, implicitly, in comparison to those elsewhere in the UK.

In addition, logistic regression analysis with backward stepwise entry of predictor variables was used to 'predict' patterns of individual participation (for more on this see Gorard *et al.* 1999b). The dependent variable, to be explained or predicted, is non-participation in lifelong learning (defined as those who report no episodes of education or training since full-time education) or of recent participation (defined as those who report episodes of post-compulsory education or training in the last three years, including current episodes). Some cases remain unclassified for this analysis. The independent variables, or potential determinants of participation, are entered in batches in the order that they occur in the individuals life (this is instead of the more usual procedures of either entering all variables in one step, or stepwise in the order of the amount of variance they explain).

The variables entered at birth were age, sex, ethnic group, and family language. The variables entered in the second stage were age of leaving full-time education (and the interactions of this with the 'birth' variables). The variables entered in the third phase were social class, employment status, area of residence, language in which they wish to learn, and age of children. The variables entered in the fourth phase were reported access to various technologies, including the Internet. Each stage also examined the impact of these variables in interaction. In this way, the variables entered at each step can only be used to explain the variance left unexplained by previous steps, and are selected by using the Likelihood Ratio statistic. Thanks to this novel method of analysis, which models the order of events in individual's lives, the relevant variables become valuable clues to the socio-economic determinants of patterns of participation in adult learning.

The decision whether to use qualifications as a predictor when modelling participation is a difficult one, since it is not clear how far qualifications are the outcome or the determinant of formal episodes. Many observers, having noted the strong relationship between prior qualifications and further participation, have suggested that qualification is a key determinant in an accumulation form of human capital theory (e.g. Roberts and Parsell 1990, Smithers and Robinson 1991). However, changes in participation over time mean that age alone is a good predictor of initial qualifications, and since the growth has been stronger for women than men, gender in conjunction with age is an even better one. When further personal and socio-economic background predictors are added to age and gender, levels of personal qualification are themselves accurately predictable (Gorard 1997).

There is, therefore, no reference to qualifications as potential predictors in the models that follow. However, alternative models have also been created with two levels of information about qualification (as part of the interactive fitting and criticism process, Dale and Davies, 1994). The gains in the accuracy of allocating individuals to categories of participation were negligible, although as soon as qualifications are introduced they become key predictors for participation. What happens is that qualifications simply replace, or act as a proxy for, socio-economic variables that are just as effective as predictors but which predate the qualifications in a causal chain. Put simply, qualifications are more nearly a characteristic of a pattern of participation than a cause of it.

Learners and non-participants

In the UK, 42% of cases reported a current or recent learning episode (in the past three years), 22% reported some non-recent post-compulsory education or training, and 36% reported no learning episodes since leaving full-time education. The first group is described here as 'recent learners' and the third group is described as 'non-participants'. The size of the non-participant group is similar to that reported in previous studies of lifelong learning (e.g. Gorard and Rees 2002). Around one third of adults are not, and have not been, involved in our 'learning society' – at least in terms of formal participation in adult learning episodes (but see Selwyn and Gorard 2002). Many of these are the adults that current policies are attempting to include. More specifically, this is the group that information technology, whether informally, or via organisations like *learndirect*, is intended to overcome barriers of time, place and cost for. The situation in Wales is worse than the UK overall and, as far as we can tell from the earlier figures (483 cases), getting worse over time. Only 39% of adults in Wales are current or recent learners, lower than in 1999 and lower than the UK (Table 1). 38% of adults report no later learning as adults, and this is more than in 1999 and more than the rest of the UK.

Table 1: Patterns of participation over time and place (percentage)

	UK 2002	Wales 1999	Wales 2002
Base: all respondents = 100%	4,896	482	1,000
Recent learner	42	43	39
Non-participant	36	34	38

However, as the following results emphasise, recent learners and non-participants in Wales differ from each other in other systematic ways that cast doubt on the possibility that increasing opportunities, overcoming barriers, and use of technology will provide a general solution to the problem of non-participation (Gorard 2000b). For example, reports of participation are less frequent among: older cohorts (they decline with age, Tables 2 and 3); less prestigious occupational groups (they decline with social class, Tables 4 and 5); those leaving full-time continuous education earlier; and those with lower levels of qualification. Table 3 is particularly powerful, since it shows clearly how older groups are less likely to have been involved in any learning, despite the longer time they have had to do so.

Table 2: Pattern of recent learners by age cohort (percentage)

	Total	17-19	20-24	25-34	35-44	45-54	55-64	65-74	75+
Base: all respondents in Wales = 100%	1,000	57	80	165	182	152	143	138	84
Recent learners	39	81	66	49	49	36	29	19	6

Table 3: Pattern of non-participants by age cohort (percentage)

	Total	17-19	20-24	25-34	35-44	45-54	55-64	65-74	75+
Base: all respondents in Wales = 100%	1,000	57	80	165	182	152	143	138	844
Non-participants	38	18	20	26	28	41	42	61	69

Table 4: Pattern of recent learners by social class (percentage)

	Total	AB	C1	C2	DE
Base: all respondents in Wales = 100%	1,000	151	242	250	357
Recent learners	39	53	57	33	26

Table 5: Pattern of non-participants by social class (percentage)

	Total	AB	C1	C2	DE
Base: all respondents in Wales = 100%	1,000	151	242	250	357
Non-participants	38	19	22	39	57

These tables show that total non-participation will diminish over time, because such a high proportion of 17-19 year-olds are current learners. However, the 18% of this age group not continuing with education after school are, according to previous studies, likely to remain non-participants, and many of the others are likely to be only 'transitional' learners – continuing with immediate full-time continuous education but then not being involved again. The two groups differed little in terms of ethnic background. Men and women are more nearly equally likely to be current learners, but men are less likely to be non-participants (36%:41%). Again this bears out earlier work showing that while immediate post-compulsory learning is now largely gender neutral, later-life learning is not (Gorard 2002).

The patterns of participation by age and class are reflected in the reported highest qualification of the respondents (Tables 6 to 8). Levels of qualification in Wales are generally lower than the rest of the UK. Highest lifetime qualification below NVQ level 2 is more prevalent among older age cohorts, again despite the greater time they have had. Low levels of qualification are somewhat more common among women (37%), those who left school at the earliest opportunity, and those who report being less likely to participate in the next three years.

Table 6: Pattern of highest qualification (percentage)

	None	NVQ2	NVQ3	NVQ4/5	Other/DK
Base: all respondents in Wales = 100%	33	23	12	19	8

Table 7: Pattern of no qualification by age (percentage)

	Total	17-19	20-24	25-34	35-44	45-54	55-64	65-74	75+
Base: all respondents in Wales = 100%	1,000	57	80	165	182	152	143	138	84
No qualification	33	16	14	11	17	41	41	60	74

Table 8: Pattern of no qualification by social class (percentage)

	Total	AB	C1	C2	DE
Base: all respondents in Wales = 100%	1,000	151	242	250	357
No qualification	33	12	20	32	52

The difference between Wales and the UK appears in almost every indicator of participation. Only 37% of adults in Wales report being likely to take part in a learning 'episode' in the next three years (compared to 42% in the UK). Even informal learning activities are generally less prevalent in Wales (Table 9). Much of the rest of this chapter considers why this might be so.

Table 9: Patterns of selected 'informal' learning (percentage)		
	UK	Wales
Base: all respondents = 100%	4,896	1000
Seldom visit library	65	70
Seldom visit museum	91	94
Seldom visit art gallery	94	97
Seldom visit community centre	77	72
Regularly visit community centre	13	17
Reading as main leisure activity	41	39

However, it is worth first considering one issue unique to Wales – its bilingual nature. Only 87% of adults in Wales learnt English as their 'mother tongue' compared to 93% in the UK. Of the remainder, the vast majority (10%) learnt Welsh as a child. These tend to be older, aged 35+ and most prevalent (19%) among men of the 75+ age category. They tend to live in rural areas rather than the South East of Wales, and because of their age they are more likely to be retired. All describe themselves as 'White', along with 98% of adults in Wales compared to 93% in the UK. 5% of recent learners in Wales studied Welsh in last 3 years. However the proportion wishing to learn through the medium of Welsh is far lower at 4% than the number who learnt it originally. Those wishing to learn through Welsh are, in general, not those for whom it is a mother tongue. They are younger 25-44, more female, with longer initial education and higher qualifications. In fact not one person of 995 reported lack of opportunity to learn in Welsh as a barrier to participation. This cannot be used to explain the lower figures for participation in Wales, although the terms of the Welsh Language Act clearly make it even harder than in the rest of the UK for the very small minority who wish to participate in a language other than Welsh or English.

Access to, and use of, ICT

A key argument for the impact of ICT on participation is the ability to overcome physical barriers such as travel and place through technology – a factor of particular relevance to Wales. However, this new dataset agrees with previous work in offering only limited support for the argument. Under 2% of respondents cited travel/transport as the chief barrier to their future participation. This figure is slightly better than for the UK as a whole, but has the methodological problem that the question was only asked of participants.

Twenty-six per cent expressed no interest in further learning, 15% claimed to be too old, 10% expressed no need to learn, 4% said they had not got 'around to it'. This is a total of at least 55% of non-participants who, if taken at their word, would be unaffected by access to learning opportunities via ICT. However, of the others 21% cited lack of time, 7% cost, 8% need to care for others, and 6% being too ill. All of these problems might be amenable, at least in part, to a technological solution.

Unfortunately, the patterns of learning and non-participation in terms of age and class are largely repeated in terms of access to the technology itself (Tables 10 and 11). For example, while 81% of recent learners have access to the Internet at work, none of the non-participants do. Of course, we cannot tell simply from these figures if there is a causal link here or, if there is, in which direction it flows (but see below).

Table 10: Pattern of recent learners by regular access to technology (percentage)

	Base: all respondents in Wales = 100%	Recent learners
Total	1,000	39
Digital TV	514	44
Analogue cable or satellite TV	138	43
Analogue TV	486	34
Internet (work only)	17	81
Internet at home	348	57
No Internet	626	28
No PC	517	21
No telephone	33	40

Table 11: Pattern of non-participants by regular access to technology (percentage)

	Base: all respondents in Wales = 100%	Non-participants
Total	1,000	38
Digital TV	514	32
Analogue cable or satellite TV	138	39
Analogue TV	486	45
Internet (work only)	17	–
Internet at home	348	20
No Internet	626	50
No PC	517	57
No telephone	33	49

Another common argument for the role of technology is that virtual colleges will encourage wider participation. In this survey, 15% people reported finding out about their most recent episode from friends or family, 6% from a work mate, 8% from printed publicity, 6% from newspapers, 14% from their college, 6% from a higher education institution, and 7% from a school. Only 2% (6 cases) reported using the Internet to help find out about the episode, and none at all used the UfI or *learndirect*. So the first conclusion is that the latter source of information is not widespread compared to more traditional sources.

Of the 6 cases using the Internet as a source of information about learning, 4 were male, none were in social class D/E, 4 already had some post-compulsory learning experience, none were unqualified while 4 had an NVQ3 qualification or higher, 5 were in work, all were White, 5 had access to the Internet at home, and all had a PC and a telephone. Given that no one reported using the UfI/learndirect, the technology route to post-compulsory education appears to be recruiting largely the 'usual suspects'. These are younger, employed, professional, male, qualified, already learners, who all have access to the relevant technology at home.

To a large extent the same pattern appears when we consider technology as the deliverer of the learning experience itself, rather than simply of information about learning. Of the recent learners, 26% reported studying at college, 14% in HE, 15% at work, 6% at a school, 6% at a private or employer-funded training centre, and 6% at home via books or correspondence. In comparison, 4% (16 cases) principally learnt at home using a computer, and only 1% (4 cases) learnt elsewhere using a computer – including at *learndirect* or UK On-line centres.

Of the 16 cases using a computer to learn at home, 8 were male, 8 were aged under 45, 14 social class ABC, 11 lived in urban areas, 7 had no previous post-compulsory experience, 4 had no qualifications while 6 had NVQ4/5, 6 were retired, 3 not working, all white, and 10 had access to the Internet at home. Of the 4 cases learning at an ICT centre, 3 were female, all were under 45, all social class DE, all lived in urban areas, 2 had no post-compulsory experience, none were qualified above NVQ2, all were unemployed, all white, none had access to the internet, and none had a PC. Thus, we have some evidence that the two groups are distinct. Those learning at home using a computer are more similar to those using the Internet to find out about learning – male, qualified, and professional – although perhaps a little older. On the other hand, those learning in centres are somewhat more likely to be female and less qualified.

These differences appear also in patterns of access to computers, and patterns of learning about computers themselves. Computer skills, IT and the Internet is by some way the largest single area of study for recent learners (27%). These tend to be older or very young (Table 12), less qualified, more not working (33% of this group) or unemployed (31%), and so more like those using IT in drop-in centres.

Table 12: Pattern of studying computing skills by age (percentage)									
	Total	17-19	20-24	25-34	35-44	45-54	55-64	65-74	75+
Base: all respondents in Wales who have done some learning in the last three years	394	46	53	80	89	54	41	26	5
Learners studying computing skills	27	37	9	22	30	39	23	34	45

Tables 13-15 show that Internet access itself is patterned by social class and qualification. Internet access (36%) is lower than in the UK (42%).

Table 13: Patterns of regular access to technology (percentage)

	Mobile Phone	CD	DVD	PC	Internet
Base: all respondents in Wales = 100%	70	77	24	48	36

Table 14: Patterns of regular access to Internet by social class (percentage)

	Total	AB	C1	C2	DE
Base: all respondents in Wales = 100%	1,000	151	242	250	357
Access to the internet	36	61	55	31	17

Table 15: Patterns of regular access to Internet by highest lifetime qualification

	Total	None	NVQ2	NVQ3	NVQ4/5
Base: all respondents in Wales = 100%	1,000	53	116	75	108
Regular access to the internet	36	14	43	60	57

Of those with access to the Internet the single most common use was email (23%), followed by browsing (23%) and looking for information on goods and services (6%). 7% mostly used the Internet for finding information relevant to learning or training, and 4% mostly used it for learning on- or off-line.

The long-term socio-economic determinants of participation

There is so much potential interaction between the variables in the analysis so far that I attempt to clarify at least part of the story via multivariate analyses. For example, it is clear so far that older groups and those who leave full-time education early are both less likely to have access to technology such as the Internet. But older groups are also more likely to have left full-time education early, and it is unclear what the inter-relationship is here. The analysis concerns those who are recent learners and those who are non-participants. The variables are entered into the analysis in the order that they would occur over the lifecourse, and are used to try and predict in which of the two groups each individual will be in.

Using only those variables known about each individual at birth the model is 67% successful in allocating them to being recent learner or not (Table 16). The only variable retained is the age cohort (sex and language of the home, for example, are not relevant once age is taken into account). Older individuals are, as we have seen above, far less likely to be learners than non-participants. For example, the youngest cohort is 44 times more likely to be learners than the older cohort.

Table 16: Success in predicting learners at birth

	Predicted not learning	Predicted recent learner
Observed not learning	240	156
Observed recent learner	96	281

[Tables 16-19 show the number of cases that can be correctly classified in terms of their actual recent learning history using only information from their past. In each table there are 773 cases (the non-participants plus the recent learners. Table 16 shows that 240+281 (67%) of these have been correctly classified on the basis of age alone].

By the time of leaving full-time education, the model for recent learners is 75% accurate (Table 17), and now includes age (as above) and age of leaving full-time education (an individual is 1.2 times as likely to be a learner with every year of immediate post-compulsory education)

Table 17: Success in predicting learners at school

	Predicted not learning	Predicted recent learner
Observed not learning	276	120
Observed recent learner	73	304

When adult and work-related variables are added, the model for recent learners becomes 78% accurate (Table 18). The determinants are age, age of leaving full-time continuing education, and now social class. The more prestigious the social class the more likely the individual is to be a learner. For example, those in social class AB are 3.2 times as likely (once other factors are accounted for) to participate as class DE.

Table 18: Success in predicting learners as adults

	Predicted not learning	Predicted recent learner
Observed not learning	307	89
Observed recent learner	82	295

Finally, when current access to technology variables are added, the model for recent learners becomes 81% accurate (Table 19). The determinants are as above, with the addition of access to technology. While regular access to mobile phone (.98), CD (.67) and DVD players (1.1) make little difference, having access to the Internet increase the odds of participation by 9.0 compared to having no access to technology at all.

Table 19: Success in predicting learners via ICT

	Predicted not learning	Predicted recent learner
Observed not learning	326	70
Observed recent learner	74	303

Several conclusions can be drawn from this simplified trajectory analysis. First, despite missing information about family background, it is clear that long-term social, economic and educational factors are closely related to patterns of current/recent learning. While access to ICT is largely patterned in the same way, access to ICT does not, in itself, add much more to our predictive model. It is, like qualifications, largely a proxy for the other, more complex, variables that pre-date it.

Conclusion

Clearly non-participation in education remains a significant and deep-rooted trend in Wales with or without ICT based initiative. That 39% of individuals reported taking part in some form of learning over the past three years is tempered by the converse finding that an equivalent proportion of the population reported no learning episodes since reaching compulsory school-leaving age. Crucially, the data reiterate the conclusion that whether or not an individual participates in learning is a lifelong pattern, already presaged at school leaving age, and intrinsically related to long-term social, economic and educational factors.

It also follows from the regression analysis of the participation data that access to ICT does not, in itself, make people anymore likely to participate in education and (re)engage with learning. Access to ICT continues to be largely patterned according to long-term pre-existing social, economic and educational factors. Thus, like educational qualifications, access to ICT is a proxy for the other, more complex, social and economic factors that pre-date it rather than as a direct contributory factor in itself. This point is an important one and worth reiterating as it is at odds with much contemporary educational thinking and rhetoric. This is highlighted in the following newspaper report on the preliminary analysis of *same* survey data:

"'Divide is Blamed for a Slump in Adult Learning'… the digital divide is having a big impact in preventing more adults from accessing new skills and learning opportunities… Inability to access the internet is a factor in encouraging more people to start studying again. … More that two thirds of people without internet access at home said they are unlikely to learn in the future, compared to less than half of those connected to the web" (South Wales Echo, 2002)

The data from the NIACE survey may not accurately reflect all informal learning that people are likely to be using ICT for. There was considerable evidence that the learning episodes reported by participants were likely to take the form of basic or advanced ICT skills courses. There was also emerging evidence that some non-participants are being 'won over' by ICT-based learning. The emergence of a small number of (relatively) older women from lower socio-economic groups beginning to learn to use IT in community-based sites does point to a change in the pattern of learning activity directly attributable to IT. What the longer-term effects of such groups 'dipping their toe in the water' of adult learning in this way remains to be seen. It is a sign of hope. Indeed, ICT skills courses could be seen as the typing and secretarial courses of the 2000s but the fact remains that such provision has replaced and not augmented other types of provision. Indeed, set against the high expectations set up by the government I can only conclude that ICT is not having the widespread beneficial impact that many politicians and educators would have us believe.

From a political point of view, politicians and policy-makers need to resist the tendency to over-play what is on offer to learners via ICT. Much of this so-called 'new' ICT-based educational pro-vision is either repackaged 'old' educational provision and courses or a narrow provision of new courses. As Cullen *et al.* (2002) quite sensibly concluded, "the evidence does not suggest the 'new learning technologies' imply or precipitate 'new forms of learning'". The majority of learndi-rect's 800 specialist courses have been in basic and advanced IT skills and tied into existing learn-ing providers such as further education colleges – hardly the cornucopia of diverse learning opportunities (anything) being made available 'anytime' and 'anywhere'. Over the last three years (practically the whole life of the UfI) 14 people out a national sample of nearly 6,000 have found out about, or arranged, a learning experience through it. That represents around 0.002% of the population, who are, in any case, merely the 'usual suspects'.

References

Cullen, J., Hadjivassiliou, K., Kelleher, J., Sommerlad, E. and Stern, E. (2002) *Review of Current Pedagogic Research and Practice in the Fields of Post Compulsory Education and Lifelong Learning* Report submitted to the Economic and Social Research Institute, London, Tavistock Institute

Dale, A. and Davies, R. (1994) *Analyzing Social and Political Change: A casebook of methods*, London, Sage

ETAG (1998) *An education and training action plan for Wales: Consultation*, Cardiff, The Education and Training Action Group for Wales

Gorard, S. (1997) *Initial Educational Trajectories*, Working paper 8, Patterns of participation in adult education and training, Cardiff, School of Education

Gorard, S. (2000a) *Education and Social Justice*, Cardiff, University of Wales Press

Gorard, S. (2000b) Adult participation in learning and the economic imperative: a critique of policy in Wales, *Studies in the Education of Adults*, 32, 2, 181-194

Gorard, S. (2002) Robbing Peter to pay Paul: resolving the contradiction of lifelong learning, *Research in Post-compulsory Education*, 7, 2, 123-132

Gorard, S. and Rees, G. (2002) *Creating a learning society*, Bristol, Policy Press

Gorard, S., Rees, G. and Fevre, R. (1999a) Patterns of participation in lifelong learning: do families make a difference?, *British Educational Research Journal*, 25, 4, 517-532

Gorard, S., Rees, G. and Fevre, R. (1999b) Two dimensions of time: the changing social context of lifelong learning, *Studies in the Education of Adults*, 31, 1, 35-48

Gorard, S., Fevre, R. and Rees, G. (1999c) The apparent decline of informal learning, *Oxford Review of Education*, 25, 4, 437-454

Gorard, S., Rees, G. and Selwyn, N. (2002) The 'conveyor belt effect': a re-assessment of the impact of National Targets for Lifelong Learning, *Oxford Review of Education*, 28, 1, 75-89

Harrison, R. (1993) Disaffection and Access in J. Calder (ed) *Disaffection and Diversity – overcoming barriers to adult learning*, London, Falmer

Lewis R. (1993) *Leaders and Teachers. Adult education and the challenge of labour in South Wales 1906-1940*, Cardiff, University of Wales Press

McGivney, V. (1993) Participation and Non-participation: a review of the literature in R. Edwards, S. Sieminski and D. Zeldin (eds) *Adult Learners, Education and Training*, London, Routledge

Roberts, K. and Parsell, G. (1990) *Young People's Routes into UK Labour Markets in the Late 1980s*, ESRC 16-19 Initiative occasional papers 27, London, City University

Roll, R. (1995) Foreword, in Tiffin, J and Rajasingham, L. (Eds.) *In Search of the Virtual Class: Education in an Information Society*, London, Routledge

Sargant, N. (1997) *The learning divide*, Leicester, NIACE

Selwyn, N. and Gorard, S. (2002) *The information age: technology, learning and social exclusion in Wales*, Cardiff, University of Wales Press

Smithers, A. and P. Robinson (1991) *Beyond Compulsory Schooling – a numerical picture*, London, Council for Industry and Higher Education

South Wales Echo (2002) 'Divide is Blamed for a Slump in Adult Learning' *South Wales Echo*, 15th May, p.27

Tight, M. (1998) Lifelong learning: opportunity or compulsion?, *British Journal of Educational Studies*, 46, 3, 251-263

Titmus, C. (1994) The scope and characteristics of educational provision for adults, in Calder, J. (Ed.) *Disaffection and Diversity. Overcoming barriers to adult learning*, London, Falmer

CHAPTER SIX

Changing and persisting patterns: the public and lifelong learning in Scotland

Professor Maria Slowey, Director of Adult and Continuing Education, University of Glasgow

Introduction

> In the understandable rush to establish new structures and getting them to function smoothly, to set ever tougher targets, to drive up the quality of teaching and learning, to involve more non-traditional learners in education and to develop more appropriate funding regimes, the main purpose of these worthy activities can easily be forgotten: we aim to create learners, young and old, who have a genuine love of learning; who have been imbued with a creative discontent and so wish to improve society for the benefit of all. (Coffield, 2002, p 6)

Much of the thinking behind the western enlightenment view of education is that it forms a key mechanism by which we learn to generalise and transcend our personal experience. According to this perspective, the best educational processes are those in which the views we derive from our personal experiences are continuously challenged in debate and by research findings. Without diving into deep waters it is always particularly interesting when the two appear to coincide – when the outcomes of social science research appear to confirm widely held common-sense views. The issue of relevance here is the relationship between *participation* and *learning*.

If research confirms what we know from personal experience, that participation does not necessarily equate with learning, and if our main interest is in learning, why do we care so much about analysing patterns of participation? Part of the answer in the past was that one of the distinguishing characteristics lay in the voluntary nature of participation by adults in education and training. The impact of a policy perspective based on a worldview of the knowledge economy which links skill enhancement to employability has however led to an identification of tendencies towards increasing levels of compulsion. Does this make the rationale underlying participation studies consequently less compelling?

For two main reasons the answer to the question about the importance of participation studies must resoundingly be in the affirmative. Firstly, while participation may not be a sufficient condition for learning, it is a necessary one. People do of course learn all the time in a myriad of ways

– hence the use of very inclusive definitions inevitably leads to the situation described by Tight (1998) when "…you probe individuals about their experiences, and enable them to label some of their disparate activities as learning – teaching them that this term actually covers things other than formal education or training – it is actually quite difficult to find non-participants." (p. 115) However if we wish to avoid the theoretical and practical morass into which this equation of learning with the whole of life leads, then the primary focus of our attention must be on those opportunities which are amenable to influence through public policy.

It is the second reason however which is of more direct relevance to the present discussion. Participation in education continues to be associated with – if not a key determinant of – important economic, social and personal benefits. The causal relationships are complex and the timescales lengthy. From an equity perspective therefore it remains essential to gather as much information as possible to assist in deepening our understanding of the familiar, but still central issues – who participates in what forms of learning opportunities, and why?

Despite the policy emphasis on lifelong learning, it is quite remarkable how the focus of most post-school participation data collection remains firmly fixed on the formal sectors of further and higher education. For over a decade the regular surveys undertaken by NIACE have provided one of the few sources of quantitative material which utilise an inclusive definition of participation, providing indicative data about motivations, communication channels and pathways of participation for the population as a whole. The survey also usefully covers all the countries and regions of the UK offering an opportunity for some preliminary comparisons.

The NIACE survey conducted in 2002 included 475 respondents from Scotland within the total weighted sample of 4,896. (For methodological details see appendix 1). A preliminary analysis of the data for Scotland is provided here as a precursor to a detailed exercise. This offers a tantalising glimpse of trends which point to both continuities and important changes in the involvement of the public in lifelong learning in Scotland.

Participation profiles

Table 1 shows an active engagement in some form of structured learning over the past three years by a significant minority of respondents from Scotland. (See Appendix 6 for details of the definition of learning used in the NIACE surveys). One quarter defined themselves as currently being engaged in learning while just under one fifth said they had recently (within the last three years) been involved.

Table 1: Participation in learning since leaving full-time education: Scotland compared to the UK (2002)

	UK %	Scotland %
Base: all respondents = 100%	4,896	475
Current learning	23	25
Recent learning (in last 3 years)	19	19
Past learning (more than 3 years ago)	21	21
None since leaving full-time education	36	34
Don't know	1	1
Total engaged in current/recent learning	42	44

In total, 65% of the Scottish sample have undertaken some form of structured learning since leaving full-time education. This percentage is considerably higher than the 42% found by the Munn and MacDonald (1988) in what remains one of the largest studies on adult participation in education and training in Scotland, involving 1,826 respondents. However, the definition of an adult returner utilised in that study (must be aged 20 or over and have had at least a two-year break from initial full-time education) was more constrained than that used by the NIACE surveys and so it cannot necessarily be assumed that participation in adult learning in Scotland has increased in the past 15 years. In addition, their definition of education and training ("any kind of study or training, or attended any classes including hobbies or personal interest classes… [lasting] in total for 7 hours or more") was perhaps more restricted than that used in the current survey and makes it difficult to directly compare findings.

The figures in Table 2 are however comparable, and they do certainly suggest that a real growth in participation by adults in learning in Scotland has taken place in recent years. Taking the results of the NIACE surveys over a 12-year period at face value they point to a dramatic increase in levels of participation in Scotland in recent years. In 1999 recorded levels of participation were amongst the lowest for all UK regions while in 2002 they are amongst the highest, and higher than the overall UK average.

Table 2: Reported levels of current and recent participation in learning by respondents in Scotland compared to the UK (1990-2002)

	2002	1999	1996	1990
Scotland	44	33	38	22
UK	42	40	40	39

Source for 1990-1999 figures: Sargant (2000) Table 12.
Note: the same question was used each year to identify participation in learning. The same sampling methodology was also employed.

Various attempts have been made to explain the apparent paradox of why traditionally higher staying on rates for initial levels of education (including further and higher education) in

Scotland have not, in the past, seemed to be associated with correspondingly higher levels of participation by adults in continuing learning – particularly through the work of John Field and Tom Schuller. In the qualitative study which followed the 1999 NIACE results it was suggested that the divergence in expected patterns (high levels of initial education leading to higher levels of participation by adults) in the case of Scotland largely "…disappeared on closer inspection, with higher IE [initial education] achievement dwindling and the appearance of lower CE [continuing education] participation resulting from different reporting habits – in itself an interesting cultural feature." (Schuller and Field, 1999, p69)

Are we really seeing a major rise in learning amongst adults in Scotland as the NIACE survey results suggest? If so this is obviously a significant trend to be welcomed and to be further studied. Certainly education has enjoyed a particularly high profile in Scotland since the establishment of the Scottish Parliament in 1999. While some of the more unrealistic expectations which accompanied the establishment of the Scottish Parliament have been moderated, it still retains a great deal of popular support. Opinion polls for example, show that the proportion who thought that the Parliament had achieved "a lot" since its establishment doubled between September 2000 and February 2001 from 11% to 25%, while the majority thought it had achieved "a little" (McCrone, 2001).

The relatively short space of time since the establishment of the Parliament and the Scottish Executive has witnessed the production of an impressive range of policy papers and associated initiatives relating to different dimensions of post-compulsory education and training – commencing notably with the Independent Committee of Inquiry on Student Finance (the "Cubie" Committee). (See for example, Scottish Executive 2001a, Scottish Parliament, 2002). Could it be that these policy developments may already be associated with positive outcomes in terms of higher participation levels? What other factors may be involved?

There is indeed some other evidence of proportionately higher levels of demand in Scotland for post-compulsory education than other parts of the UK – for example, applications to higher education increased sharply by 3.8% compared to just 1% in the rest of the UK. (UCAS, 2001) On the other hand issues about adult learning have tended to be implicit or addressed on a sectoral basis, although the theme of lifelong learning has underpinned a range of policy areas associated not only with education and training but also economic development, social inclusion, urban and rural regeneration. (See for example, the reports of the Centre for Research in Lifelong Learning and Slowey, 2002)

As we see below, the workplace is one of the main sites of learning for people in Scotland as elsewhere. We might therefore have expected some of the increases to be reflected through Labour Force Survey results – however in 2000 the figures for those in employment who reported that they had engaged in some form of job-related training over a four week reference period were very similar to the UK as a whole – 14% as opposed to 15%. Further work would also need to be undertaken to see if the profile of the sample from Scotland had any bearing on the findings as it contained a slightly higher proportion with higher levels of qualifications than the UK total (27% as opposed to 24% with degree/HE/SVQ 4/5; 17% as opposed to 12% with highers/SVQ level 3) on the other hand, at the other end of the scale a slightly higher percentage had no qualifications (27% as opposed to 31%).

Overall, however, at first sight there do appear to be grounds for cautious optimism that new patterns of adult involvement in lifelong learning may be emerging in Scotland.

We now turn our attention to finding out more about who these learners are – and who they are not in terms of educational background, gender, social class and age groups. Here, regrettably, the patterns highlight persisting rather than changing patterns in relation to the learning divide in Scotland.

Educational background

Current and recent learners were significantly more likely to have higher qualifications – 43% of current/recent learners compared to only 14% of those who had not undertaken recent learning had a degree or equivalent qualification. In contrast, almost 40% of those with no recent learning had no qualifications compared to only 11% of current/recent learners. Although the proportions differ, this is a similar trend to that found in all participation study – participants in adult learning are more likely than non-participants to be well qualified. As McGivney (2002) comments in her recent review of surveys on participation "…as a whole, participants in organised learning are no more representative of the whole population than they were 10 years ago. There has been growth in participation but less "breadth"." (p17)

Table 3: Adult learning participation patterns by the highest qualifications held by respondents in Scotland		
Highest qualification	No recent learning %	Current/recent learners %
Base: all respondents in Scotland = 100%	264	211
None (< O level)	39	11
GCSE/SVQ2	25	17
Higher/SVQ3	14	22
Degree/HE/SVQ4-5	14	43
Other	3	4
Don't know	4	3

Qualifications held are still very closely correlated with age completing full-time education so Table 4 shows very similar patterns of participation. Three-quarters of those with no recent learning finished full-time education at age 16 or under compared to only 42% of current/

recent learners. A quarter of the latter group stayed in full-time education until aged 21 or over; this compares with just 8% of those with no recent learning.

Table 4: Adult learning participation patterns by school leaving age of respondents in Scotland		
Age finished full-time education	No recent learning %	Current/recent learners %
Base: all respondents in Scotland = 100%	264	211
16 or under	75	42
17-18	12	22
19-20	4	3
21or over	8	26
Still full-time student	0	8

Gender

In relation to gender, as the figures in Table 5 show, a slightly higher proportion of women than men had undertaken recent learning (46% to 42%) but slightly more women than men had not taken any learning since leaving full-time education (36% to 32%).

Table 5: Adult learning participation patterns by gender of respondents in Scotland			
	Total %	Men %	Women %
Base: all respondents in Scotland = 100%	475	230	245
Current learning	25	22	28
Recent learning (in last 3 years)	19	20	19
Past learning (more than 3 years ago)	21	24	17
None since leaving full-time education	34	32	36
Don't know	1	0	1
Total engaged in recent learning	44	42	46

Social class

In terms of the social class profile of learners in the formal sector of post-compulsory education, the figures for Scotland do appear slightly better than those for other parts of the UK. The extent however to which expansion has resulted in any redistribution of opportunity remains the subject of much debate. On the one hand, Lindsey (2002) drawing particularly on data from the Scottish School Leavers Survey suggests that there is evidence that those from working-class backgrounds are increasingly likely to participate in further and higher education.

"The main policy prerequisite of gradually eroding inequalities is therefore not targeted initiatives of the higher education funding councils, or in the more general kind embodied in the introduction of comprehensive secondary schools. These may help some individuals, may stimulate disadvantaged groups to raise their aspirations, and – above all – may encourage an existing trend towards overall expansion. But the necessary requirement for significantly reducing inequality over the last half century has simply been overall expansion." (Lindsey, 2002)

However, significant inequalities remain, and the link between education and economic mobility appears to be a contributory factor across the UK to an actual *fall* in intergenerational economic mobility (for both men and women) over the last 40 years (Blanden 2002). A comparative analysis based on detailed information from two large data sets (the National Child Development Study and the British Cohort Survey) found that by the year 2000 the income levels achieved by those born in 1970 were determined by the income levels of their parents "to a significantly higher extent" than was the case for those born in 1958. (Blanden *et al.*, 2002) and differential levels of participation in formal post-compulsory education were identified as important contributory factors to this reduction in economic mobility.

Whether or not simple expansion of opportunities assists in widening access for adults the fact remains that, as Table 6 indicates, social class – or more correctly – socio-economic status (SES) as a proxy for social class) is strongly associated with levels of participation. Almost half of those who had not currently/recently participated in learning were in SES group DE (47%) as opposed to 15% of those from social groups AB.

Table 6: Adult learning participation patterns by social class of respondents in Scotland		
Social class	No recent learning %	Current/recent learners %
Base: all respondents in Scotland = 100%	264	211
AB	15	29
C1	19	30
C2	20	18
DE	46	23

Intergenerational inequalities

Here again, there appears to be little evidence of change from earlier surveys. Current/recent learners were significantly more likely to be in the younger age groups – 58% of current/recent learners were under 44 years of age compared to 34% of those who had not engaged in learning over the previous three years. As younger adults will have had greater opportunity to benefit from the expansion of initial education (into which definition it is increasingly appropriate to include direct progression to further and higher education) this points not only to a continuing intergenerational learning divide but also to a divide which is potentially increasing.

Table 7: Adult learning participation patterns by age of respondents in Scotland		
Social class	No recent learning %	Current/recent learners %
Base: all respondents in Scotland = 100%	264	211
17-19	3	12
20-24	3	11
25-34	12	17
35-44	16	18
45-54	18	20
55-64	22	12
65-74	16	6
75+	10	3

Why and what do people wish to learn?

In relation to subject matter, given the common nature of much of the economic and social infrastructure, it is not surprising that the patterns for Scotland mirror almost exactly those for the UK as a whole. The most popular subjects of recent learning were IT related activities including computer skills and learning about the internet (22%). Other professional and vocational qualifications featured as the second highest category (11%).

Table 8: Main subjects pursued by current and recent learners		
Subjects studied by at least 5% of current/recent learners	UK %	Scotland %
Base: all current/recent learners = 100%	2,073	211
Computer skills/IT/Internet	24	22
Other professional and vocational qualifications	11	11
Health and medicine including nursing and first aid	6	6
Foreign languages	4	5
Other academic subjects	6	5
Other 'leisure' subjects	4	5
Business Studies/administration/marketing	5	4

Motivation to learn is complex and multi-layered. Respondents however were asked to give what they felt were the main reasons why they wished to engage in learning. As the summary in Table 9 shows, in total, work-related reasons for undertaking the learning were most common (60%), followed by personal development reasons (48%). These reasons appear to reflect the profile of subjects in Table 8 above. Slightly less frequent were education or progression reasons (42%) and these were less important to Scottish respondents than to those in the UK as a whole (49%). Indeed, as the more detailed breakdown in Table 10 indicates, only 15% of Scottish learners compared to 24% of those in the UK as a whole gave 'to get a recognised qualification' as a main reason. It would be interesting to investigate this finding further – as we saw earlier, the profile of the sample from Scotland included somewhat higher proportions with higher levels of qualifications than the UK total but also a slightly higher percentage who had no qualifications (27% as opposed to 31%).

Table 9: Summary of main reasons for starting current/recent learning

Main reasons	UK %	Scotland %
Base: all current/recent learners = 100%	2,073	211
Work related	58	60
Personal development	52	48
Education/progression	49	42
Not my choice	6	5
Don't know	2	1

The most frequently cited reasons for participation were interest in the subject (35%) and the enjoyment of learning (30%), and because it would help in their current job (29%). The issue of growing compulsion to participate in continuing education/lifelong learning is one which had been gaining growing attention in recent years. As Table 10 indicates around 5% of the sample in Scotland regarded themselves as being in this category. It would seem important to undertake further analysis around areas such as the outcomes and completion rates for such participants – not to mention their likely interest in further learning.

Table 9: Summary of main reasons for starting current/recent learning

Main reasons	UK %	Scotland %
Base: all current/recent learners = 100%	2,073	211
Work related	58	60
Personal development	52	48
Education/progression	49	42
Not my choice	6	5
Don't know	2	1

Table 10:Details of main reasons for starting current/recent learning

Items mentioned by at least 1% of Scottish recent learners	UK %	Scotland %
Base: all current/recent learners = 100%	2,073	211
I am interested in the subject/personal interest	34	35
I enjoy learning/it gives me pleasure	31	30
To help in my current job	26	29
To develop myself as a person	25	19
To get a job	17	17
To get a recognised qualification	24	15
To make my work more satisfying	13	14
To get a rise in earnings	8	8
To improve my self-confidence	12	7
To get a job with a different employer	5	6
To change the type of work I do	8	6
To help me get onto a future course of learning	6	5
To meet people	8	4
To get promotion	7	3
Not really my choice – employer requirement	4	3
As a result of participating in another activity	3	2
Not really my choice – professional requirement	2	1
Not really my choice – benefit requirement	0	1

When and where do people engage in learning?

In relation to duration of learning, over half were undertaking learning which lasted for the significant period of more than one year – Scottish students were slightly less likely (54%) to be undertaking learning of this duration than the UK total (58%). This contrasts with the Munn and MacDonald study which found only 23% of returners had taken a course lasting more than one year (1988). Learning of less than one month was slightly more common amongst Scottish learners (13%) as opposed to the total (9%).

Table 11: Hours a week spent on learning by current/recent learners

Hours per week	UK %	Scotland %
Base: all current/recent learners = 100%	2,073	211
Up to 3	29	26
4-6	19	20
7-9	9	8
10-12	9	8
13-15	4	5
16-20	9	6
21-30	10	14
31-40	8	9
41+	3	4
Don't know	1	–
Mean	12.79	14.23

The workplace (21%) and FE college (21%) were the two most frequently mentioned locations for learning. One distinctive feature is the role of the workplace as a site of learning which was more common in Scotland (21%) than the UK as a whole (15%) – despite, as mentioned earlier, Labour Force Survey results not appearing to suggest any higher incidents of job related learning in Scotland than other parts of the UK. One of many interesting avenues for further empirical work however would be to assess the possible impact of initiatives such as the Scottish Union Learning Fund (the STUC affiliated unions contain over 630,000 members), the Ministerial Trade Union Working Group on Lifelong Learning and the role of the Enterprise Agencies.

Table 12: Main location of current/recent learning

Locations mentioned by at least 5%	UK %	Scotland %
Base: all current/recent learners = 100%	2,073	211
Where I work	15	21
FE college	21	21
University/OU	16	14
At home – informal learning/from a book	6	8
At home – using a computer, CD-ROM, Internet	6	6
At home – correspondence or open learning	3	6
Adult education centre/WEA	7	4
Employer's training centre	5	3

Access and barriers to learning

Around a quarter of respondents did not have to pay any fee for their learning activity – or up to one third, if employer provided in-house courses are taken into consideration. Of those liable for some form of fee respondents were most likely to have paid them personally. Undertaking learning funded through government sources was twice as common among the Scottish respondents (10%) than UK learners as whole (5%) – which may not be unassociated with the finding that more respondents in Scotland had heard of the European Social Fund than the UK total (37% and 28% respectively). Given the fact that around 4% of all respondents were full-time students it would be interesting to know the extent to which the formal abolition of fee payment for higher education in Scotland may also have had some bearing.

Table 13: Sources of financial support for fees for current/recent learning

Mentioned by at least 5% of recent learners	UK %	Scotland %
Base: all current/recent learners = 100%	2,073	211
No fees to pay	28	24
Myself	33	29
Employer/potential employer paid outside fees	14	15
Employer funded provision of learning	7	10
Other government funding	5	10
Family/relative	6	2

The financing of adult participation in learning has always represented a complex patchwork and now lifelong learning is, as Field puts it "…one of several policy areas where there is a new balance of responsibilities between individuals, employers and the state." (2000, p 220) As Table 14 indicates over a quarter cited travel and equipment costs. However, half of all those currently/recently engaged in learning said they had incurred no other costs. Two possible interpretations present themselves. Either it could mean that the real costs are borne elsewhere – by employers, by voluntary organisations or by the state or local authorities via, in the main, educational institutions. Or it could relate to the use of sources of learning which may appear to respondents as being in some manner cost neutral.

Table 14: Other costs associated with current/recent learning

Mentioned by at least 5% of current/recent learners	UK %	Scotland %
Base: all current/recent learners = 100%	2,073	211
No other costs	50	50
Travel costs	31	31
Cost of equipment	28	27

Further analysis is required to ascertain just who is receiving what kinds of support for learning. To take just one example, as Table 15 indicates, women were more likely than men to have paid the fees themselves or to have drawn on some form of government funding. Men were likely to have had their fees paid by their employers. These findings are of some concern as the New Earnings Survey shows that women's earnings in Scotland are on average 54% those of men and even for *full time workers* remain on average 75% those of men. (Office for National Statistics, 2000)

Table 15:Sources of financial support for fees for current/recent learning in Scotland,		
Main funders only	Men %	Women %
Base: all current/recent learners in Scotland = 100%	98	113
Myself	22	34
Family/relatives	2	1
Employer	18	12
Employer-funded provision	12	9
Other government	6	12

In relation to other barriers, when asked about ease of access or otherwise to their place of learning, three-quarters of all respondents said they found it "easy" to get to the place of learning and a further fifth did not have to travel at all because they were either learning at home or in the workplace. One striking difference between Scotland and elsewhere is the high proportion of learners in Scotland who said they were currently/recently learning either at home or work (22%) compared to the UK as a whole (13%). This may account for the fact that, despite the difficulties of rural access in Scotland, slightly fewer reported themselves as finding it "difficult" to get to their place of learning than the total (5% as opposed to 7%).

Channels of communication

Prior to the establishment of the Scottish Parliament the Scottish Office had identified educational guidance as important to raising aspirations and increasing participation. The Scottish Executive has viewed the establishment of *sufi* (Scottish University for Industry) and *learndirect* as key mechanisms for delivering guidance. In fact only 1% of respondents actually mentioned *learndirect* explicitly as a source of information. Adult education guidance networks continue to operate (variably) at local levels across Scotland but their role also appears to be limited compared to the key role played by word of mouth.

Table 16 suggests there may be some interesting differences in information flows and channels of communication between Scotland and other parts of Britain which would merit further investigation.

Table 16: Source of information about main subject of current/recent learning

Items mentioned by at least 1% of Scottish current/recent learners	UK %	Scotland %
Base: all current/recent learners = 100%	2,073	211
Work employer, training office, personnel	20	17
Friends/family	13	14
Workmates/colleagues	12	14
Newspapers/magazines	7	13
Colleges	11	9
School	7	8
University/OU/HE	7	3
Community centre/voluntary group	2	3
Public library	2	3
Job centre, job club	2	3
Printed publicity elsewhere	2	2
Careers service, guidance service	2	2
Internet/www/online	2	2
Printed publicity delivered to home	3	1
Trade union/professional association	1	1
Learndirect	1	1
TV	1	1
Adult education centre/WEA	4	0
Other	7	9
Don't know	2	4

Learners in Scotland most commonly heard about their most recent learning activity through their employers (17%), work colleagues (14%), friends and family (14%) or newspapers and magazines (13%). Interestingly in relation to the latter, newspapers and magazines were mentioned twice as often as sources of information in Scotland (13%) compared to the UK as a whole (7%) suggesting a potentially interesting area for further investigation on the role of the print media in different parts of the UK.

Outcomes of learning

Scottish learners were a little more likely than UK learners as a whole to give the course up before the end (10% compared to 5%). One can only speculate on why this might be but it is possible that since fewer were working towards recognised qualifications, course completion was less important.

Scottish respondents were more likely than those in the UK as a whole to say that there had not been any benefits (22% compared to 16%). Interestingly, the three benefits cited by more than one-fifth of Scottish respondents were all concerned with personal and social development rather than vocational development, even though in Table 9 above, work-related reasons were the most common cited reasons for having undertaken the learning. It does, however, tally with the predominance of the individual personal-related reasons given in Tables 9 and 10. The lesser importance of qualifications to the Scottish learners was again evident in that over a fifth of UK learners but only just over a tenth of Scottish respondents mentioned gaining a qualification as one of the benefits.

Table 17: Changes or benefits as a result of current/recent learning	UK %	Scotland %
Base: all current/recent learners = 100%	2,073	211
My self-confidence has improved	29	25
I have developed myself as a person	29	23
I have met new people/made new friends	26	23
I have been helped/expect to be helped in my current job	14	19
I enjoy learning more	19	17
My work has become/I expect my work to become more satisfying	15	12
I have got/expect to get a recognised qualification	21	11
I have got/expect to get a promotion or rise in earnings	9	8
I have changed/expect to change the type of work I do	7	7
I have got/expect to get a job	13	6
My health has improved	4	5
My children/family have become more interested in learning	4	5
I am more involved in local events and issues	5	5
I have got/expect to get a job with a different employer	5	4
I have moved/expect to move onto a further course of learning	6	3
None	16	22
Don't know	2	1

Future Plans

More than half of Scottish respondents said that they were unlikely to take up learning in the next three years and just over a third thought it likely.

Table 18: Likelihood of taking up learning in next 3 years		
	UK %	Scotland %
Base: all respondents = 100%	4,896	475
Likely	41	37
Unlikely	57	58
Don't know	3	5

When those who said they thought they were unlikely to engage in learning were asked why, the two main reasons given were 'not interested' and 'work/time pressures'. This is similar to other studies, including Munn and MacDonald where the authors suggested that this was a depressing view because it implied that non-participants tended to view 'adult education and training as intrinsically uninteresting, not worth giving time to'. (1988) They contrasted that with the view of returners who saw participation in learning as useful and interesting. A notable finding in the current survey is that these reasons were less likely to be given by non-participants in Scotland than by the total UK respondents (18% of those in Scotland and 25% of UK respondents cited lack of interest and 17% and 20% respectively mentioned time pressures). However it is important to note that over one fifth of respondents in Scotland did not give any reason.

Table 19: Main factors likely to prevent respondents engaging in learning in the future		
Items mentioned by at least 5% of recent learners	UK %	Scotland %
Base: All respondents not likely to take up learning in the next 3 years = 100%	3,820	383
Not interested/don't want to	25	18
Work/other time pressures	20	17
I feel I am too old	13	15
I feel no need to learn anymore	9	10
Childcare/caring responsibilities	7	8
I haven't got round to doing it	6	8
Cost	7	6
I am too ill/too disabled	4	5
None	15	21

The reason 'time pressures' could as noted in other surveys be used a socially acceptable euphemism for 'not interested', especially given the frequent finding that adults with many interests and hobbies are more likely to also participate in learning despite having so many demands on their time. The reason 'I feel I am too old ' is an interesting one which is being tackled at grassroots level by community organisations such as Age Concern and local authority sponsored projects.

A worrying factor from the perspective of concerns about growing learning divisions, is the fact that current/recent learners were four times more likely than those with no recent learning to say that they were likely to take up learning in the next three years (64% compared to 16%) and far less inclined to say that it was unlikely that they would do so (30% compared to 80%).

Table 20: Future plans by learning profile of respondents in Scotland

Likelihood of taking up learning in next 3 years	No recent learning %	Current/recent learners %
Base: all respondents in Scotland = 100%	264	211
Likely	16	64
Unlikely	80	30
Don't know	4	6

A higher proportion of women (42%) than men (33%) said that they were likely to take up learning in the next three years. Of those who said that they were unlikely to take up learning in the next three years, men were more likely than women to say that they were not interested or that work/time pressures prevented them.

Table 21: Future plans by sex of respondents in Scotland

Main reasons preventing learning	Men %	Women %
Base: All respondents in Scotland not likely to take up learning in the next 3 years = 100%	189	193
Not interested	24	13
Work/time pressures	22	12
I feel I'm too old	12	16
I don't feel the need to learn	12	8

Views of the public on learning, education and training

Respondents were asked their views on a range of statements about education and training. Around three-quarters of respondents agreed that learning was enjoyable for its own sake (79%) and that people who got training tended to find their jobs more interesting (72%). Almost two-thirds also agreed that people who trained at work ended up with better promotion or better pay (63%). Agreement with these statements suggests that the majority of respondents have a very positive view, both of learning as an end in itself and as a means of improving the quality of one's working life. It was also interesting that such a high proportion (69%) felt confident about learning new skills. This implies that non-participation is not necessarily a result of fear or inability to learn.

Table 22: Views on education and training

	Agree		Neither agree nor disagree		Disagree	
	UK %	Scotland %	UK %	Scotland %	UK %	Scotland %
Base: all respondents = 100%	4,896	475	4,896	475	4,896	475
Learning is enjoyable for its own sake	81	79	12	15	6	4
People who get training find their jobs more interesting	73	72	16	18	8	7
I am confident about learning new skills	74	69	10	11	15	18
People who get trained at work end up with better promotion or better pay	65	63	18	20	13	15
I don't see why I should pay for learning that is to do with my job or career	47	49	21	18	29	28
There is not enough help/advice about the different sorts of learning people can do	37	37	17	18	42	40
People should not be expected to learn new skills for their career in their own time	32	32	19	18	47	48

Around half agreed that they should not have to pay for learning which was to do with their job or career, although over a quarter disagreed with this. This question was slightly ambiguous however and could have been interpreted in different ways – was the learning to which it referred to do with developing a new career with a different employer (as in undertaking a full-time course) or in developing skills that were needed by the current employer? It's more likely that people would be willing to pay for the former than for the latter. A similar ambiguity is present in the statement about learning new skills for their career in their own time. Almost half of respondents disagreed with this and around a third agreed.

Respondents were almost equally divided about whether or not they agreed that there was not enough advice about the different sorts of learning that people could do. With over a third feeling that there was not, this implies that much more help and guidance needs to be made available.

Role of new technology

The potential (hype?) of ICT to increase access and hence participation levels in structured learning opportunities is frequently accompanied by concerns about the digital divide – as typified in the Scottish Executive Report, *Digital Inclusion* (2001b). "Today in Scotland, access to the Internet is growing, and growing quickly. Figures for 2000 show that almost 25% of all Scottish households are online, an increase of some 10% on the figures for 1998. For these people, this will open a world of opportunity in work, in education, in leisure and in business". [Paragraph 2, references excluded] The Report proceeds to point out that the figure of 25% is lower than that for the UK as a whole which is estimated at 33% and to focus attention on those sections of the population in danger of being left out.

As shown above, IT related activities remain one of the most frequently mentioned topics for current/recent learning in Scotland (22%) and for future learning plans (18%). This suggests that these are the areas which tend to be supported by employers but also that they are areas about which many people wish to learn more. Half of all respondents had access to a computer and more than a third to the internet – higher, it seems than the average for Scotland. However, this means that half of the population were unable to access computer-based learning at home and that almost two-thirds were not able to use one of the fastest growing sources of information – the internet

Table 23: Technology to which respondents had regular access

	UK %	Scotland %
Base: all respondents = 100%	4,896	475
CD player	79	79
Mobile phone	71	70
Computer/PC/laptop	53	50
Net: any Internet	41	39
Internet via normal phone line	39	36
DVD player	26	25
Internet via Broadband connection	5	5
None	12	13

When one looks at the main purpose for which the Internet was used, e-mail stands out as being the most common (37%). The only other main purpose for which over a tenth of respondents used it was general browsing or surfing. However, when one looks at Internet use in general, the picture is a little more positive. Although, again, the most common activity for which the Internet was used was e-mail, over two-thirds also used it for general browsing or surfing (much of which might be described as learning). In addition, over a third used it for finding information for their learning or training, a quarter used it for finding information related to their children's schoolwork and a quarter used it to learn on or off-line. On other matters, one interesting difference between Scotland and the rest of the UK relates to use of the internet for personal banking – 23% as opposed to 31% respectively. A finding which is perhaps not unrelated to the fact that a (slightly) lower proportion of the population in Scotland actually hold a bank account? (Independent Committee of Inquiry on Student Finance, 1999)

Table 24: General and main activities for which internet was used	Used Internet for in general		Used Internet for mostly	
	UK %	Scotland %	UK %	Scotland %
Base: all respondents with internet access = 100%	2,006	187	2.006	187
Using e-mail	76	74	37	37
General browsing or surfing	69	69	21	21
Finding information about goods and services	58	52	7	6
Buying or ordering tickets, goods or services	43	40	2	4
Finding information for my learning/training	38	35	6	8
Downloading software	30	26	2	3
Downloading or playing music	27	26	1	1
Finding information related to children's schoolwork	23	25	3	4
Learning on/off-line	22	25	2	1
Using or accessing government or official services	24	25	1	1
Personal banking, financial and investment activities	31	23	3	1
Looking for jobs or work	26	21	1	1
Using chat rooms	16	17	1	3
Other things	8	3	2	0
None/Don't know	8	9	9	9

The public and learning in Scotland – some key issues from a preliminary analysis of the NIACE survey

This initial glimpse at the data from Scotland throws up some interesting patterns which require further exploration. These include:

- Findings which suggest there has been significant growth in recent years in overall levels of participation by adults in learning in Scotland;

- The fact that, even using a generous definition of participation in learning, one third of respondents in Scotland have not engaged in any form of structured learning since leaving initial education;

- The significance of the workplace in a wide variety of ways – as a site of learning, as a source of information on learning opportunities, as a motivating factor for learning;

- The persistence of social class and initial educational background in shaping opportunities and attitudes to learning;

- The existence – and potential acceleration – in intergenerational inequalities in relation to participation opportunities;

- The significant inequalities in the levels of support – particularly financial – available to women compared to men;

- The implications for policy of the fact that current/recent learners were four times more likely than those with no recent learning to say that they were likely to take up learning in the next three years.

The summary UK report on the 2002 survey by Fiona Aldridge and Alan Tuckett is entitled *Two steps forward, one step back*. The comparative figures presented here suggest an appropriate title for the forthcoming companion report on Scotland may in fact be *Three steps forward, one step back?*

Notes

* I am extremely grateful to Carolyn MacDonald for her invaluable assistance in extracting some of the data for respondents in Scotland.

1. Characteristics of sample from Scotland compared to total sample.		
	UK %	Scotland %
Base: all adults aged 17 or over	4,896	475
Sex		
Male	49	48
Female	51	52
Age		
17-19	5	7
20-24	7	7
25-34	18	14
35-44	20	17
45-54	15	19
55-64	14	18
65-74	12	12
75+	8	7

1. Characteristics of sample from Scotland compared to total sample (continued).

	UK %	Scotland %
Social class		
AB	19	21
C1	29	24
C2	22	19
DE	31	36
Children in household		
None	67	64
0-4 years	13	13
5-15 years	26	29
Working status		
Full time	41	38
Part time	12	13
Unemployed	4	4
Not working	15	15
Retired	24	26
FT student	4	4
Access to services		
Digital/satellite/cable	48	49
Cable/satellite not digital	18	20
Analogue TV only	52	51
Internet work only	3	3
Internet at home	42	40
No internet	54	56
No PC	47	50
No phone	3	4

1. Characteristics of sample from Scotland compared to total sample (continued).

Highest qualification held	Total %	Scotland %
Base: all adults aged 17 or over	4,896	475
None (< O level)	31	27
GCSE/NVQ2	25	21
Higher/NVQ3	12	17
Degree/HE/NVQ4-5	24	27
Other	5	4
Don't know	3	4

2. Analysis of subjects pursued – UK

- *Gender:* Women were more likely than men to be studying Health and Medicine (9% compared to 4%). Men were more likely to be studying Business Studies (26% compared to 22%), Computer Skills (26% compared to 22%) and Engineering (7% compared to 0%).

- *Age:* Older adults were more likely than other age groups to be studying Arts (13% of over-65s, 7% of 55-65 – but only 3% of total). Business Studies was most popular among the younger age groups (12% of 20-24 years olds, 8% of 17-19 year olds). Computer Studies was most popular among the 35-64 year olds (17-19 years – 10%, 20-24 – 12%, 25-34 – 23%, 35-44 – 29%, 45-54 – 32%, 55-64 – 31%, 65-74 – 25%, 75+ – 18%); Foreign languages were most popular among older age groups (55-64 – 7%, 65-74 – 8%, 75+ – 11%).

- *Age:* Not surprisingly, older groups were more likely than the younger ones to be taking 'other leisure subjects' (10% of the 55-64 and 9%, 65-74, 13% of 75+) while, in contrast, the younger groups were more likely to be taking 'other academic subjects' (13% of 17-19 and 12% of 20-24); those in their mid-twenties to mid-forties were more likely to be engaged in learning connected to other professional and vocational qualifications (17% of 25-34 and 13% of 35-44).

- *Social Class:* [Looking at any differences that are at least 3% different from the overall total or 5% between groups] – Computer Studies was least popular among the AB group and most popular with the C1 group (21% of AB, 27% C1, 23% C2, 25% DE); Other professional and vocational qualifications were more common among the C1s and C2s (9% of AB, 12% C1, 13% C2, 8% DE).

3. Note re qualifications

As a methodological point it should be noted that the options in Scottish FE qualifications in this survey were slightly out of date as respondents were asked whether they were aiming for SCOTVECs instead of SQA qualifications. It is unlikely that this has had a great effect on the responses although it is possible that the number indicating that they were working towards BTEC/SCOTVEC equivalents would have been higher if SQA units had been included.

References

Aldridge, F. and Tuckett, A. (2002) *Two steps forward, one step back: the NIACE Survey on Adult Participation in Learning 2002*, Leicester, NIACE

Blanden, J. (2002) 'Mobility has fallen', *CenterPiece*, Vol.7, No.2, pp 8–13.

Blanden, J., Goodman, A., Gregg, P. and Machin, S. (2002) *Changes in Intergenerational Mobility in Britain* (Discussion Paper No. 517) London, Centre for Economic Performance, London School of Economics.

Coffield, F. (2002) *A New Strategy for Learning and Skills: Beyond 101 Initiatives*, Newcastle upon Tyne, Department of Education, University of Newcastle.

Field, J. (2000) "Learning in the Isles: evolving policies for lifelong learning in the Republic of Ireland and the United Kingdom" in J. Field and M. Leicester (eds.) *Lifelong Learning: Education Across the Lifespan*, London and New York, Routledge Falmer.

Independent Committee of Inquiry on Student Finance (1999) *Student Finance: Fairness for the Future (The "Cubie" report)*, Edinburgh, Independent Committee of Inquiry.

McCrone, D. (2001) "Opinion Polls in Scotland", *Scottish Affairs*, No. 37, Autumn, pp 26–33.

McGivney, V. (2001) *Fixing or Changing the Pattern? Reflections on widening adult participation in learning*, Leicester, NIACE

Munn, P. and MacDonald, C. (1988) *Adult Participation in Education and Training* (Practitioner MiniPaper 4), Edinburgh, Scottish Council for Research in Education.

Office for National Statistics (2000) *New Earnings Survey*, London, The Stationery Office.

Paterson, L. (2001) *Education and Inequality in Britain* (Paper prepared for the British Association for the Advancement of Science, Glasgow 4 September), Edinburgh, Institute of Governance, University of Edinburgh.

Sargant, N. (2000) *The Learning Divide Revisited: a report on the findings of a UK-wide survey on adult participation in education and learning*, Leicester, NIACE

Schuller, T. and Field, J. (1999) "Is there divergence between initial and continuing education in Scotland and Northern Ireland?", *Scottish Journal of Adult and Continuing Education*, Vol.5, No.2, pp 16–76.

Scottish Executive (2001a) *Lifelong Learning: A Summary Review of Scottish Executive Documents and Action over the Past 2-3 years*, Edinburgh, Scottish Executive.

Scottish Executive (2001b) *Digital Inclusion Strategy: Connecting Scotland's People*, Edinburgh, Scottish Executive.

Scottish Office (1998) *Opportunity Scotland*, Edinburgh, Scottish Office.

Scottish Parliament (2002) *Enterprise and Lifelong Learning Committee Interim Report on Lifelong Learning, Edinburgh*, The Stationery Office.

Slowey, M. (2002) "Evidence Based or Evidence Ignored? Progress of the Lifelong Learning Agenda in Scotland" in F. Grey (ed.) *Lifelong Learning and Higher Education: The Next Phase*, Cambridge: Universities Association for Continuing Education, Occasional Paper No. 26.

Tight, M. (1998) "Bridging the Learning Divide: the nature and politics of participation", *Studies in the Education of Adults*, Vol.30, No.2, pp110–119.

Tuckett, A. and Sargant, N. (1999) *Marking Time: The NIACE survey on adult participation in learning 1999*, Leicester, NIACE

CHAPTER SEVEN

Learning in adult life in Northern Ireland: the turning of the tide?

Professor John Field, Director of Academic Innovation and Continuing Education,
University of Stirling

The condition of adult learning in Northern Ireland seems to be thriving. For much of the twentieth century, participation rates in Northern Ireland have been among the lowest in the UK (Field 1994; Field 1997; Sargant 2000). This low participation pattern has been clear in the NIACE surveys, but was also found in other large-scale surveys as well (Field 1999). The 2002 survey suggests that there has been a dramatic rise in participation, to the extent that Northern Ireland is now approaching similar levels to those found in England and Scotland, with Wales now providing the sole remaining laggard among the four main nations of the UK. It would be wrong to place too much weight on data drawn from one survey along, but the 2002 results point to a significant change that demands explanation.

As elsewhere in the UK, government policy in Northern Ireland since 1997 has placed a high priority on lifelong learning. A consultative paper on lifelong learning for all was issued in the wake of David Blunkett's Green Paper for England and Wales (Department for Education and Training 1998). Subsequent measures undertaken by the devolved Northern Ireland Executive have focused particularly upon attempts to engage excluded and non-participant groups in learning, and the expansion of continued upskilling of the workforce (Department for Employment and Learning 2002). Sean Farren, Northern Ireland's first Minister for Employment and Learning under the devolved administration, devoted considerable attention to lifelong learning, both in public and private, before shifting to Finance and Personnel in an executive reshuffle in December 2001. Before 1997, adult learning was virtually ignored by government. Subsequently, it has been treated increasingly as a decisive tool in the regeneration of the Northern Ireland economy, and the creation of a socially just community – both widely viewed as essential in the transition from violent conflict.

This chapter analyses some of the main findings of the 2002 survey for Northern Ireland. A few qualifications should be entered at the very outset. First and foremost, it is only possible to analyse the Northern Ireland data at the most general level. The unweighted sample of 167 is relatively

---

[1] This chapter has benefited from discussion at the Lifelong Learning Forum organised by Paul Nolan at Queen's University, Belfast.

small, and any further subdivision within that overall number will produce figures that are too small to allow for any trustworthy conclusions to be drawn. Of course, Northern Ireland is a small place; its population is less than three per cent of the UK total, and the weighted sample reflects that. Resources were not made available for a boosted sample (of the kind used in the survey in Wales), and therefore a detailed analysis of the kind that can be undertaken for the rest of the UK is simply not possible for Northern Ireland. Moreover, for the same reason, the possibility of sampling error is also higher in the case of Northern Ireland. Finally, the survey is confined to the UK, and it could be argued that this is not the only sensible basis for comparison. There is currently no evidence on participation in the obvious comparator nation, namely the Republic of Ireland. We should therefore treat these findings as a prelude to further, more systematic investigation in the future, rather than viewing them as unambiguous evidence that the tide has turned.

With these qualifications in mind, the chapter sets out to consider the following questions about patterns of participation in adult learning in Northern Ireland as compared with the rest of the UK:

- What does the survey tell us about broad trends in participation in adult learning?

- What do the findings have to say about patterns of participation?

- To what extent is the development of e-learning likely to produce further changes?

While the chapter focuses particularly on the evidence respecting Northern Ireland, the analysis addresses more general concerns that

Context

A series of previous studies has shown that on a range of measures, levels of adult learning in Northern Ireland have long fallen behind the rest of the UK. The 1996 NIACE survey showed that levels of general adult participation in learning were the lowest of any UK region (Field 1997a); participation in work based training was low (Field 1999); adult participation in higher education was also relatively low (Field 1997b); average levels of performance against standardised tests for literacy and numeracy were relatively low (Sweeney, Morgan and Donnelly 1998). This performance is all the more remarkable given that academic attainment in Northern Ireland's school system outstrips that of almost all other UK regions. To illustrate this claim, in 1999-2000 almost 38% of school pupils in Northern Ireland achieved 2 or more A-level passes, as against 30% for the UK as a whole (McGinty and Williams 2001, 56). Generally, as is well known, there is a strong association between initial educational achievement and learning in adult life. The Northern Ireland pattern was therefore quite unusual in showing a divergence between high levels of initial achievement and low levels of adult participation.

Attempts to explain this pattern drew attention to structural factors such as those arising from the idiosyncrasies of Northern Ireland's labour market, the structures of the wider economy and the organisation of schooling, all of which were held to dampen down demand (Field 1999). There has also been interest in cultural factors, in particular the importance of informal mechanisms for promoting the transmission of information and skills, associated with the strength of family and neighbourhood ties, as well as the vibrancy of the community based sector as an alternative to official educational institutions (Field and Spence 2000). These explanations essentially emphasised a failure of demand, and implied that the underlying causes were deep-rooted.

In addition, it has been suggested that there was an inherited lack of policy attention, arising from a long history of relative neglect (Field 1994). Until the mid-1990s, it was common for inward investment agencies to claim that a highly skilled workforce was one of the key factors attracting overseas employers to locate in Northern Ireland. Since the later 1990s, however, policy makers have paid considerable attention to the promotion of lifelong learning in Northern Ireland, and this process intensified under the devolved administration. Such initiatives as UfI/learndirect, Individual Learning Accounts and the New Deal for adults were essentially localised versions of UK-wide measures. The European Commission has also shifted attention and investment towards lifelong learning, partly by prioritising lifelong learning within the Structural Funds and partly by directing funds towards community based learning through the Special Support Programmes for Peace and Reconciliation. Within Northern Ireland, there has also been a lively debate over lifelong learning and skills acquisition in the Assembly, and under Sean Farren and his success Carmel Hanna, the Department of Employment and Learning has given a new, high profile to lifelong learning from the outset. The devolved administration has also generated a series of measures of its own (including the expansion of adult guidance and the launch of a coherent basic skills service). Taken together, these steps mark an about-turn of the previous pattern of policy neglect.

The 2002 findings: broad trends

The 2002 survey suggests that levels of participation in Northern Ireland are still below those found in Scotland and England, but have for the first time overtaken Wales (Table 1). This finding has of course to be seen in the light of the limitations of a single snapshot with a limited sample. Nevertheless, given the scale of the gap found in previous surveys, it represents a significant change on previous years, and indeed is the first evidence of any convergence between Northern Ireland and the rest of the UK.

Table 1: Adult learning in the UK nations, 2002

	N Ireland	Scotland	England	Wales
Base: all respondents = 100%	144	475	4,036	241
Any recent learning	40	44	42	39
None since leaving full time education	45	34	35	39

Northern Ireland was included in two previous NIACE surveys, allowing for comparisons to be made over time (Table 2). The findings suggest considerable growth in participation, particularly in the last three years. Moreover, while the growth has been UK-wide, the rate of change in Northern Ireland is well above average. In 1999, for example, the gap between England and Northern Ireland amounted to nine percentage points; by 2002, it had fallen to two percentage points. However, the survey also confirms that the proportion of complete non-learners is higher in Northern Ireland than elsewhere. While only 36% of all respondents across the UK claimed that they had not studied or learnt since leaving full time education, this category accounted for 45% of respondents in Northern Ireland. The proportion saying that they were unlikely to take up any learning in the next three years, at 60%, was also the highest of any UK region other than East Anglia. Among the group who thought themselves unlikely to take up learning, 27% in Northern Ireland cited lack of interest as the main barrier, which was just above the UK average. In this respect, then, little has changed since previous surveys so far as non-participation is concerned.

Table 2: Adult learning in Northern Ireland, 1996-2002		
	Base: all respondents in Northern Ireland = 100%	Current/recent learning
2002	144	40
1999	143	32
1996	511[2]	28

Patterns of participation

The survey provides some evidence with respect to the patterns of adult learning. It confirms that the pattern of learning in Northern Ireland shows a number of distinct features, and contrasts in several respects with the situation elsewhere in the UK. There are some areas of the survey, though, where the limited size of the sample makes it risky to claim that the findings are of value (this rules out, for example, an analysis of the spread of subjects and qualifications pursued by adult learners in Northern Ireland).

Learners in Northern Ireland are distinctive in the location for their learning (Table 3). Compared with the rest of the UK, the workplace is relatively unimportant in the part it plays in adult learning (and it is notable that among the barriers cited by non-learners, anticipated difficulty in getting time off work was cited by 12% in Northern Ireland, as against only 3% across the UK). Equally, the survey confirms that community based centres are more important in Northern Ireland than elsewhere, and it also indicates that both the home and the new technologies are more important in Northern Ireland.

---

[1] In the 1996 survey resources were made available for a boosted sample.

Table 3: Main location for learning

	N Ireland	Scotland	England	Wales
Base: all current/recent learners = 100%	58	211	1,711	94
Main location = where I work	6	21	15	15
Main location = FE college	20	21	21	25
Main location = HE institution	26	14	16	15
Main location = community centre	5	2	3	3
Main location = at home (OL course)	–	6	3	2
Main location = at home (SDL)	8	8	6	4
Main location = at home (new ICTs)	12	6	6	4

The data also appear to suggest that higher education is also very important in Northern Ireland. However, these responses may be partly misleading, given that the main further education institutions are also publicly known as higher education providers (a fact reflected in the widely used title Institute of Further and Higher Education). What can be said with confidence is that respondents appears to be studying disproportionately in academic settings and community centres, and are less well represented in workplaces.

Adult learners turn to a wide range of sources of information about learning opportunities (Table 4). For Northern Ireland, the survey confirms earlier evidence of the importance of informal sources of information in decisions about learning. The media by contrast are relatively unimportant at present. Notable findings include the central role of family and friends, and the importance of employers and workmates for Northern Ireland learners. The survey also confirms that there is a continued role for print publicity from institutions in reaching learners in Northern Ireland. It also highlights the complete failure of careers services to reach adult learners, not only in Northern Ireland but also across the UK.

Table 4: Main source of information about learning

	N Ireland	Scotland	England	Wales
Base: all current/recent learners = 100%	58	211	1,711	94
Work/employer	20	17	21	20
Workmates/colleagues	16	14	12	7
Newspapers/Magazines	7	13	7	6
FE College	4	9	11	14
Brochure, poster	12	3	5	8
Careers/advice service	–	2	2	3
Family/friends	34	14	13	15

Learners' aims in studying appear broadly to mirror those found elsewhere in the UK (Table 5). However, there are some distinctive emphases:

- qualifications are generally important for learners across the UK;

- significant numbers are studying without any regard to qualifications, but no more than in England and Wales and fewer than in Scotland;

- Northern Ireland learners are more likely to be aiming at a degree, suggesting a rather academic bias in overall patterns of learning.

The survey also suggests that Northern Ireland learners are less likely to be working towards vocational qualifications. Given the limited role for qualifications in an economy dominated by small firms, who recruit and appoint more through personal connections and reputation than through formal means, this may be understandable. However, much attention has been paid to skills deficits in specialist craft and technician areas, and inward investors are less likely to be able to rely on personal knowledge than are well-established firms.

Table 5: Main qualification aim of learners

	N Ireland	Scotland	England	Wales
Base: all current/recent learners = 100%	58	211	1,711	94
None	32	41	33	33
A/Highers	1	1	3	6
Bachelors degree	17	7	12	9
HNC/D	4	9	2	2
N/SVQ	4	11	10	12

Learners in Northern Ireland were much more likely to point to changes that had happened as a result of their learning. Only 6% in Northern Ireland could not identify any changes in their lives as a result of their learning, against 16% in England and 22% in Scotland. And there were further distinctive features to be noted in the extent to which learners had experienced specific changes:

- NI learners were much more likely to value the new friends they had made through learning (42% as against 26% in England and 23% in Scotland);

- NI learners were much more likely to say their work had become more satisfying as a result of their learning (36% as against 15% for the UK as a whole);

- NI learners were more likely to believe that they had developed as a person (38% as against 29% UK-wide)

- NI learners were most likely to value the confidence they had gained from learning (36% in NI against 29% UK-wide)

- NI learners were far more likely to say they enjoyed learning more as a result of doing some previous learning (30% as against 19% UK-wide).

Broadly, then, learners in Northern Ireland appear to gain more from their learning than elsewhere in the UK, and this is as marked for personal development (including self-esteem) as for more instrumental gains. This may, of course, be at least partly a function of the type of learning that has been undertaken, and as we have already seen there is a strong tendency in Northern Ireland to academic forms of learning, with comparatively high proportions taking part in higher education. The emphasis on friendship and sociability is consistent with earlier findings on the importance of social networks in adult learning in Northern Ireland (Field 1999).

The survey also sought to shed light on adults' attitudes to learning (Tables 6 and 7). Most people across the UK share extremely positive views on learning in adult life, but there were some small differences between the nations. In particular, people in Northern Ireland were most likely to see learning as leading to positive outcomes for work, yet there is less acceptance in Northern Ireland that individuals should be willing to give up free time for their own career development, and fewer people than elsewhere in the UK accept that they should fund learning that is to do with their job or career.

Table 6: Future aims of respondents in near future				
	N Ireland	Scotland	England	Wales
Base: all respondents = 100%	144	475	4,036	241
Future learning likely	39	37	41	37
Future learning unlikely	60	58	56	59

Table 7: Attitudes towards learning in the UK nations				
	N Ireland	Scotland	England	Wales
Base: all respondents = 100%	144	475	4,036	241
Agree that "Learning is enjoyable for its own sake"	77	79	81	84
Agree that "I am confident about learning new skills"	72	69	75	73
Agree that "People who get training find their jobs are more interesting"	78	72	73	75
Agree that "People who get trained at work end up with better promotion or better pay"	78	66	65	60
Agree that "There is not enough help or advice available about the different sorts of learning"	39	37	37	40
Agree that "People should not be expected to learn new skills for their career in their own time"	37	32	32	29
Agree that "I don't see why I should pay for learning that is to do with my job or career"	52	49	46	48

The potential of e-learning

It has been widely suggested that online technologies represent a means of overcoming barriers to access. In the case of Northern Ireland, the new communications technologies could potentially be of enormous significance in making online learning available to remote and rural communities, and to those working in small firms and family enterprises. They might also play a part in overcoming physical barriers to movement within the major urban centres, and helping to promote communication on a cross community basis. Stephen Gorard and Neil Selwyn among others has expressed significant misgivings about the extent to which technological means can actually help overcome what may be deeply rooted cultural, social and economic barriers to participation (Gorard and Selwyn 1999). Does the 2002 survey shed much light on the potential of e-learning in Northern Ireland?

The 2002 survey included three questions concerned with access to and use of the internet. One of these was concerned with the main use of the internet, but because the numbers responding are mainly low the results have been ignored in this paper. Other questions dealt with the extent of regular internet access, and with the various uses that respondents had experienced at some stage.

Some 40% of the Northern Ireland sample claimed to have regular access to the internet, which is broadly comparable to the figure for England (and higher than the levels reported for Scotland and Wales). This finding contrasts with evidence from official survey data, which tend to place Northern Ireland among the UK regions with particularly low levels of home access to the internet. For example, according to the most recent Expenditure and Food Survey (previously the Family Expenditure Survey), only 31% of Northern Ireland households have access to the internet, a similar proportion to Wales and the north East of England but well below the levels for the rest of England and for Scotland (Office for National Statistics 2002, 3). While this apparent discrepancy may reflect a potential sampling error, it could also point to higher than usual levels of internet access outside the home (for example, in community centres, workplaces and educational institutions), to Northern Ireland's higher than average family size, or to a combination of these factors.

The survey also asked individuals how they had used the internet. In using the internet for personal communications, the Northern Ireland sample tended to respond in largely similar ways to respondents in the rest of the UK. Roughly the same proportion of people with internet access in Northern Ireland had made some use of email (72%) and chatrooms (18%). There are also very similar proportions who had used the internet to help with their children's homework, or access public services. In terms of commercial usage, the Northern Ireland sample behaves in significantly different ways from respondents in the rest of the UK. It is much more likely to have used the internet to find out about goods and services, to buy things, and to play or download music, but rather less likely to download software. When asked what their main use was, there were some differences between Northern Ireland respondents and people elsewhere.

By contrast, e-learning is less common among the Northern Ireland respondents. The proportion of adults with internet access who had used the internet for learning in Northern Ireland is 19%, below the UK average of 22%. Some 31% had used it to find information about learning, as against 38% across the UK. Superficially, then, these findings appear to support the broadly sceptical view of the internet's potential for extending access in a region that has significant levels of geographical barriers to learning. But this is to ignore evidence of a remarkable degree to which people in Northern Ireland are apparently embracing the internet as a way of accessing other goods and services. What is notable is then the limited progress made by government initiatives such as the Grid for Learning and UfI in tapping into this enthusiasm. Rather than confirming the internet's limited value as a tool for accessing learning, then, the findings suggest considerable potential, as yet untapped, for growth.

Conclusions

Two-fifths of adults in Northern Ireland are either learning something now or have done so in the recent past. These figures represent a considerable shift from those reported in earlier NIACE surveys, and they could be taken to imply that Northern Ireland has moved some distance on the way to becoming a learning society. Of course, it is possible that these findings arise at least in part from problems with the sample in the survey. Yet it is striking that the 2002 findings are consistent with earlier studies when it comes to other features, such as the persistence of high rates of non-participation, the importance of informal networks, and the low profile of the workplace. If it is too early to claim that the tide has turned, the survey points to a faster current running in favour of lifelong learning than has been found in the past. Although it is not possible to explain with confidence precisely why this shift has occurred, it has taken place at a time when policy makers have taken a number of steps to promote lifelong learning. For those who take the view that there is a direct connection between lifelong learning and the prosperity and social cohesion of a society, this is a very positive message.

There are some continuing signs of weakness. The survey suggests that work based learning has lagged behind, with employers providing comparatively limited opportunities for workplace learning. Vocational qualifications are attracting few takers. Rather, Northern Ireland learners are often working towards academic qualifications, which may reflect a recent expansion of opportunities for adults to study in higher education, but poses difficult questions about the balance between the demand in the labour market for graduates and the interests of learners. People are less willing to give up their own time or money to fund their learning than is the case in Britain. Careers advisory services have yet to engage effectively with adults in search of information about learning. There is also evidence that the potential of e-learning is considerably greater than current take up levels might suggest.

The survey also offers important pointers to strengths that can be built upon. To select the most obvious, these should include the generally positive attitudes of people towards adult learning, the high value placed upon workmates and friends as a source of reliable information about learning, and the strong benefits that learners associate with their learning. The home and community centres play a very important role as places where learning takes place, offering possibilities of strengthening opportunities for progression into a wider range of learning activities. In short, the message for policy makers and providers is that adult learning in Northern Ireland has come a long way since the mid-1990s, but much still remains to be done. These are important messages for policy makers and others who believe that lifelong learning is a key element in creating a knowledge based economy and inclusive society.

References

Department for Education and Training (1998) *Lifelong Learning: a new learning culture for all*, Stationery Office, Belfast

Department for Employment and Learning (2002) *Essential Skills for Living. Equipped for the future: building for tomorrow*. Stationery office, Belfast

Field, J. (1994) Policy-borrowing and adaptation in the development of continuing education in Northern Ireland, 1921 – 50, in *Cultural and Intercultural Experiences in European Adult Education*, ed. S. Marriott & B. J. Hake, University of Leeds, 34-52.

Field, J. (1997a) Northern Ireland, in N. Sargant *et al*, *The Learning Divide: a study of participation in adult learning in the United Kingdom*, NIACE/DfEE, Leicester, 91–8.

Field, J. (1997b) Access or Equity? Adults in higher education in Northern Ireland, *Journal of Access Studies*, 12, 2, 139–52

Field, J. (1999) Schooling, Networks and the Labour Market: explaining participation in lifelong learning in Northern Ireland, *British Journal of Educational Research*, 24, 4, 501–15.

Field, J., and Spence, L. (2000) Informal learning and social capital, in F. Coffield (ed.), *The Necessity of Informal Learning*, Policy Press, Bristol, 32–42

Gorard, S. and Selwyn, N. (1999) Switching on the Learning Society? Questioning the role of technology in widening participation in lifelong learning, *Journal of Education Policy*, 14, 5, 523–34

McGinty, J. and Williams, T. (2001) *Regional Trends No. 36: 2001*, Stationery Office, London

Office For National Statistics (2002) *Internet Access: households and individuals*, National Statistics, London

Sargant, N. (2000) *The Learning Divide Revisited*, NIACE, Leicester

Sweeney, K., Morgan, B., and Donnelly, D. (1998), *Adult literacy in Northern Ireland*, Northern Ireland Statistics and Research Agency, The Stationery Office, Belfast.

CHAPTER EIGHT

Match or mismatch: do the findings reflect the qualitative evidence?

Veronica McGivney, Principal Research Officer, NIACE

There is much in the 2002 NIACE survey that is consistent with existing evidence of adult learning patterns and trends. The gap in participation between different social groups; the decrease in participation with age; the importance of the workplace as a site for learning and the mostly informal ways in which people find out about organised learning opportunities – all of these echo the findings of previous surveys and studies of adult participation. The evidence from qualitative studies, however, suggests that the survey may underestimate the actual numbers of current and recent learners.

Under-reported learning

It is very difficult for any national survey to capture with pinpoint accuracy the full range and complexity of adult learning patterns. Much depends on how people self-report and this is where the problem lies. Qualitative studies frequently find that, however broad and inclusive the definition of learning supplied, some individuals fail to mention the less formal learning activities in which they have engaged, even when these include structured courses, because they do not regard them as 'proper' or 'serious' learning. I first came across this tendency some years ago in discussions with participants in a range of non-accredited WEA courses. The learners involved unanimously and with some passion refused to describe what they were doing as learning, largely it seemed because it was enjoyable and bore little relation to compulsory formal education (McGivney, 1990). Other studies have since encountered the same phenomenon. For example, researchers investigating community attitudes to education and training found that some individuals who claimed not to be engaged in any form of education or training were actually participating in community-based non-accredited courses or other learning activities in organisations where the main remit was not education (Bowman *et al*, 2000).

Despite the relatively comprehensive definition of learning used in the NIACE survey, therefore, it is possible that respondents have tended to refer mainly to formal learning episodes that have taken place in dedicated learning environments. This inference is reinforced by the fact that 37 per cent of current and recent learners reported learning in higher education institutions, further education colleges and tertiary or Sixth form colleges and only 13% in community and leisure centres, adult education centres, evening institutes, WEA classes, informal groups, voluntary organisations, health and fitness clubs – all places where a considerable amount of purposeful adult learning takes place. It could be that some people still find it difficult to reconcile less formal learning activities or learning that takes place in informal settings with a conception of learning as something formal and assessed that takes place in a formal educational environment:

> Formal episodes of learning such as degree courses, attendance at training colleges, formal training courses organised by the employer at work and so on tend to be immediately identified by survey respondents as learning activities, but they are less clear about including informal, unstructured types of learning. This is particularly true of some learning at work that is seen as 'just part of the job'. It is also true of some types of non-vocational learning because the purpose of the activity is seen as fun rather than learning (Edwards *et al*, 1998).

In the case of the NIACE survey, such perceptions may have been reinforced by the wording of some of the questions, for, however inclusive it sets out to be, the wording of the survey is still skewed towards the traditional, more formal education paradigm. For example, although a relatively broad definition of learning is provided, it is followed by a series of questions which ask about the 'subjects' respondents are learning about. As learning is divided into subjects at school, subjects are strongly associated with formal learning in a formal learning environment. However there are some forms of adult learning that are hard to fit into a subject-bounded category, for example, broad and exploratory second chance or New Horizons-type programmes that evolve in consultation with learners; flexible return to learn courses and the kind of activities funded by the Adult and Community Learning Fund which might include forming a choir or producing a community newspaper or video. There is also shared and collective learning related to immediate local or environmental issues that individuals might find difficult to place within specific subject label.

The repeated use of the word 'subjects' in the early questions could encourage the perception that, for the purposes of the survey, only participation in traditional, subject-based courses counts as learning. If respondents feel that what they have been learning cannot be described as a 'subject', then they might well question whether it can be defined as learning at all. It is not surprising, given this emphasis, that responses to the later question (20) on what people would like to learn in the future, fall mostly within the same subject categories specified in responses about the focus of their current or recent learning. Perhaps the most significant response to this question, however, is the number of 'don't knows' (38 per cent in contrast to the 17 per cent expressing interest in the most popular learning area – computer skills, Information Technology and using the Internet). As in previous surveys, 'Don't know' was the most frequent response to this question across all groups, irrespective of age, sex, ethnic origin and location. The fact that many people do not define their learning preferences in advance confirms a frequent finding of qualitative research – that adult learning is often in response to an immediate interest, need or concern arising in everyday life.

Class bias

There is another factor that may have influenced the way people responded to the survey and that may have a bearing on the social class divide in participation that it, like all of its predecessors, revealed. This is the class bias implicit in some of the wording of the survey itself.

It is possible that the initial questions asking about respondents' activities and interests may have alienated some individuals who do not lead the kind of lifestyle implied by the leisure-time options listed, many of which are strongly associated with an affluent middle-class culture. For example, the question immediately preceding the first one on learning asks how often respondents visit or go to: a public library, the cinema, theatre, concert, opera, ballet, museum, art gallery, community centre, social club or place of worship. With some exceptions (cinema, community centre, social club, place of worship) these are largely middle-class pursuits and listing them could make individuals who do not participate in such activities feel inadequate or outside the cultural norms that are assumed and, some may feel, promoted in the survey. The unfortunate placing of this list before the first question on learning could be interpreted as indicating that learning is an integral part of the same lifestyle. Some respondents may therefore have been reluctant to classify themselves as learners as this could identify them with the values and mores of a different social class. Could the proliferation of middle-class cultural references be actually reinforcing perceptions of learning as something that other people and social classes do?

The prompt lists attached to some of the other questions may also be at variance with the experience of some respondents. For example, in Question 6, respondents are asked to choose which item on a displayed list best describes their reason for learning 'a certain subject or skill'. The list excludes three of the most common reasons for returning to learning revealed in qualitative studies – to help one's children; because others in one's circle (friends, family, peer group, colleagues) are doing it, and because learning opportunities are offered in a familiar community location that people frequent for another purpose (McGivney, 1999). There is no 'other' category listed.

The amount of purposeful learning that goes on may therefore be considerably under-reported in the NIACE survey as a result of restricted understandings of the term 'learning' reinforced by the wording of some of the questions, and I would argue that both the number of recent and current learners and the breadth of potential learning interests are probably greater than the findings suggest.

Capturing less formal learning

Both the NIACE survey and the National Adult Learning Survey (SCPR, 1997) and its successors, employ broad definitions of learning, however the difficulties involved in trying to encapsulate the full range of adult learning in a 'snapshot' survey are well understood. It is extremely difficult to assess the extent of informal learning – the submerged part of the 'learning iceberg' identified by Tough (1971; 1978) several decades ago – as we tend not to recognise or describe much of the learning we do during our personal, social and working lives as 'learning', even if it is intended and structured (McGivney, 1999). In research into adult participation in learning in Wales, interview data revealed that the 31% of respondents who reported no formal learning episodes had: 'in many cases undergone transformations in their lives that would involve significant learning' (Gorard and Rees, 2002: 108).

One attempt to measure informal learning has been made in Canada (Livingstone, 1999) where a national survey explored the extent to which people engage in different forms of independent individual or collective informal learning (defined as learning without externally imposed criteria or authorised instructors) at work, in the home, in community and voluntary activities and in hobby/interest-related activities. Extrapolation from the findings suggested that Canadian adults spend about 15 hours a week in informal learning compared with 3-4 hours a week in formal learning. People with less schooling and qualifications were just as likely to be learning informally as those with higher academic achievements, and there was not the same falling off with age as there is in formal learning.

In this country there has also been a burgeoning of interest in informal learning and a number of studies on the subject have been published (see for example, Cullen *et al*, 1999; Coffield (ed), 2000). A study of the 'conceptual terrain' of non-formal learning is being conducted for the Learning and Skills Development Agency, and a large-scale, longitudinal research study of informal learning in society is planned by the University of Exeter Research Centre for the Learning Society, in partnership with the BBC and the Universities of Edinburgh and Cardiff.

Investigating the nature and extent of informal learning will not, however, eliminate the problem of non-recognition and under-reporting of learning by some survey respondents. Studies repeatedly show that it is often the word 'learning' itself that creates a block, not only for those who are outside, but also for those inside a structured learning situation. Sometimes this can only be removed by an in-depth qualitative approach. It is often found that if you ask adult learners what they have 'learnt' in a given learning situation, they will perceive this as a question about formal learning achievements to do with assessment of levels of knowledge or skill and find it difficult to answer. If you ask them what they can *do* that they could not do before, or whether they feel or act differently as a result of their learning, it is possible to get a far more detailed and informative response (see McGivney, 1998).

An in-depth qualitative approach is also an effective way of eliciting genuine learning interests and needs. As responses to surveys indicate, if you ask individuals directly what they wish to learn, they will automatically try and frame their answer within a standard educational paradigm, i.e. with reference to formal courses and programmes which instruct people in specific areas of knowledge or skills, because they believe this what the word learning implies. Some will then specify subjects that are of no real interest to them in order to give what they believe will be an acceptable response (but would not engage in such programme were they made available); others who do not consider formal education or training to be specifically relevant or of use to them, will declare a lack of interest in learning anything. A practised community education development worker will come at the question a different way and find out what people's immediate priorities, interests and concerns are and then work at translating these into relevant learning activity. If, for example, as I have found in several localities, the most immediate problem faced by poor working-class women is how to communicate anxieties about their children's health, education and development to 'people in authority', this would neither be perceived nor expressed as a learning need that could be addressed in a conventional, subject-based course. However, skilled adult and community education workers have been able to identify the potential for learning in such situations and help the women deal with their concerns by initiating informal discussion groups onto which they have gradually built structured learning activities and courses on child development, confidence-building, communication and assertiveness skills (McGivney, 1991).

One way of drawing out the full extent of adults' learning histories and interests could therefore be to take a sub-set of the original survey sample and ask them a different set of in-depth, exploratory questions which could tease out both the learning they have undertaken in the context of their everyday lives, and the kinds of learning that would be of real use and relevance to them. No method will reveal the full picture of adult participation behaviour, but a complementary qualitative approach could fill in some of the gaps and enrich our understanding of the trends revealed in the survey.

Taken on their own, the findings of the 2002 survey are generally consistent with other annual snapshots as well as confirming some important facets of adult learning that tend to be insufficiently recognised in policy. It is interesting to note, for example, that respondents considered the greatest impact of their learning to be self-development, improved confidence and social contacts, not instrumental benefits, and that over 80 per cent thought that learning was enjoyable for its own sake. This again is a common qualitative research finding. There is a wealth of evidence which shows that adult learners value the creative and intellectual stimulus, enjoyment, social interaction and increases in confidence that they gain from learning as much if not more than any education-, career- or income-contingent outcomes (see, for example McGivney 1994; Turner and Watters, 2001)

Moreover like all its predecessors, the NIACE 2002 survey highlights imbalances in participation that still need to be rectified – too few learning opportunities are being provided for older adults and there are still many people in the lower socio-economic groups who need to be convinced of the relevance and value of organised learning. The dip in participation between 2001 and 2002 reported in the headline findings of the 2002 survey (Aldridge and Tuckett, 2002), is puzzling, however and difficult to explain in relation to qualitative findings. Lack of interest, work and other time pressures are typically cited as the most frequent reasons for non-participation but whether there are other more subtle underlying reasons, only an in-depth, qualitative study might reveal.

References

Aldridge, F. and Tuckett, A. (2002) *Two steps forward, one step back: The NIACE survey on adult participation in learning 2002*, Leicester, NIACE

Bowman, H., Burden, T. and Konrad, J. (2000), *Successful Futures? Community views of adult education and training*, Joseph Rowntree Foundation/York Publishing Services

Coffield, F. (ed) (2000) *The Learning Society: The necessity of informal learning*, Bristol, the Policy Press

Cullen, J., Batterbury, S., Foresti, M., Lyons, C. and Stern, E., (1999), *Informal learning and widening participation*, London, the Tavistock Institute

Edwards, R., Raggatt, P., Harrison, R., McCollum, A. and Calder, J. (1998), *Recent Thinking in Lifelong Learning: A review of the literature*, Research Report RR80, DfEE.

Gorard, S. and Rees, G. (2002) *Creating a Learning Society? Learning careers and policies for lifelong learning*, Bristol, the Policy Press

Livingstone, D.W. (1999), *Researching expanded notions of learning and work and underemployment – findings of the first Canadian Survey of informal learning practices*, NALL, Centre for the study of Education and Work, Department of Sociology and Equity Studies, Ontario Institute for Studies in Education, University of Toronto

McGivney, V. (1990) *Education's for Other People: access to education for non participant adults*, Leicester, NIACE

1991, *Evaluation of the Women's Education Project in Belfast*, Belfast, Women's Education Project/Leicester, NIACE

McGivney, V. (1994) *Pilot survey to identify use of skills gained in adult continuing education and training courses provided by Gloucestershire LEA*, unpublished research papers, ACET, Gloucestershire LEA

McGivney, V. (1998) *Adults learning in pre schools*, PSLA/NIACE

McGivney, V. (1999) *Informal learning in the community: a trigger for change and development*, Leicester, NIACE

Social and Community Planning Research (SCPR), (1997), *1997 National Adult Learning Survey*, London, SCPR

Tough, A. (1971) *The Adult's Learning Projects*, Toronto, OISE Press

Tough, A. (1978) *The Adult's Learning Projects: A fresh approach to theory and practice*, Toronto, OISE Press

Turner, C. and Watters, K. (2001) *Proof Positive: Learners' views on approaches to identifying achievement in non-accredited learning*, Leicester, NIACE

RSGB's Omnibus survey and random location sampling method

Method

The information presented in this report was obtained as part of RSGB's General Omnibus Survey for March 2002. Appendix 6 contains a copy of the questionnaire.

Sample

The survey was based on a representative sample of c.5000 adults. They were selected from a minimum of 390 sampling points by random location method, which is described below.

Fieldwork

Respondents are interviewed at home by interviewers organised by SFR's Regional Managers according to RSGB's detailed instructions about the survey and administration procedures. The back-checking procedures that were carried out met the requirements of the Market Research Society Interviewer Quality Control Scheme (IQCS). The interviews took place during the period 13 February – 3 March 2002.

Data Processing

After coding and editing the data, weights were used to allow for sampling variation. The weighting scheme took account of the boost interviews in Wales by down-weighting the boosted region back to its normal proportion in the UK population. Details of the weighted and unweighted samples are shown in Appendix 4.

RSGB Random Location Sampling Method

A unique sampling system has been developed by Taylor Nelson Sofres for its own use. Utilising 1991 UK Census small area statistics and the Post Office Address File (PAF), the eligible area of the country has been divided into 600 areas of equal proportion. The areas within each Standard Region were stratified into population density bands, and within band in descending order by percentage of population in socio-economic Grades I and II.

To maximise the statistical accuracy of Omnibus sampling, sequential waves of fieldwork are allocated systematically across the sampling frame so as to ensure the maximum geographical dispersion.

The 600 primary sampling units are allocated to 25 sub-samples of 24 points each, with each sub-sample in itself being a representative drawing from the frame. For each wave of Omnibus fieldwork a set of sub-samples is selected so as to provide the number of sample points required (typically c.130 for 2,000 interviews). Across sequential waves of fieldwork all sub-samples are systematically worked, thereby reducing the clustering effects on questionnaires asked for two or more consecutive weeks.

Each primary sampling unit is divided into two geographically distinct segments, each containing, as far as possible, equal populations. The segments comprise aggregations of complete post-code sectors. Within each half (known as the A and B halves) postcode sectors have been sorted by the percentage of the population in socio-economic groups I and II. One postcode sector from each primary sampling unit is selected from each Omnibus, alternating on successive selections between the A and B halves of the primary sampling unit, again to reduce clustering effects. For each wave of interviewing each interviewer is supplied with two blocks of 100 addresses, drawn from different parts of the sector. Addresses are contacted systematically with three doors being left after each successful interview.

Interviewing is restricted to after 2pm on weekdays or all day at the weekend. To ensure a balanced sample of adults within effective contacted addresses, a quota is set by sex (male, female, housewife, female non-housewife)); within female housewife, presence of children and working status and within men, working status.

A guide to socio-economic class

Grade 'A' Households: the upper middle class

The head of a Grade 1 household is a successful business or professional person, senior civil servant, or has considerable private means. A young person in some of these occupations who is not yet fully established may still be found in Grade 'B', though s/he eventually should reach Grade 'A'.

In country or suburban areas, 'A' grade households usually live in large detached houses or in expensive flats. In towns, they may live in expensive flats or town houses in the better parts of town.

Grade 'B' Households: the middle class

In general, the heads of 'B' grade households will be quite senior people but not at the very top of their profession or business. They are quite well-off, but their style of life is generally respectable rather than rich or luxurious. Non-earners will be living on private pensions or on fairly modest private means.

Grade 'C1' Households: the lower middle class

In general Grade 'C1' is made up of families of small tradespeople and non-manual workers who carry out less important administrative, supervisory and clerical jobs, i.e. what are sometimes called 'white collar' workers.

Grade 'C2' Households: the skilled working class

Grade 'C2' consists in the main of skilled manual workers and their families. When in doubt as to whether the head of the household is skilled or unskilled, check whether s/he has served an apprenticeship; this may be a guide, though not all skilled workers have served an apprenticeship.

Grade 'D' Households: the semi-skilled and unskilled working class

Grade 'D' consists mainly of manual workers, generally semi-skilled or unskilled. It also includes non-earners: retired people who before retirement would have been in 'D' Grade and have pensions other than State Pensions, or have other private means.

Grade 'E' Households: those at lowest level of subsistence

Grade 'E' consists of old age pensioners, widows and their families, casual workers and those who, through sickness or unemployment, are dependent upon social security systems.

Notes on the tables

The sample covers the adult population of the United Kingdom, aged 17 and over. The sample used is specified in each table, and details of the weighted and unweighted samples are given in Appendix 4.

Figures in the tables are from the 1999 and 2002 RSGB/NIACE surveys unless otherwise indicated.

The 1980 survey was carried out by Taylor Nelson Associates; the 1990 survey by BMRB; and the 1996 survey by the GALLUP organisation.

Tables are percentaged vertically unless otherwise specified.

All tables are based on weighted totals. Researchers who wish to pursue any particular topic can obtain the necessary basic figures from the set of full analyses at NIACE.

In tables, * indicates less than 0.5 per cent but greater than zero, and − indicates zero. NSR indicates not separately recorded and NA indicates not asked.

Percentages equal to or greater than 0.5 have been rounded up in all tables (e.g. 0.5 per cent = 1 per cent, 36.5 per cent = 37 per cent).

Owing to the effect of rounding weighted data, the weighted bases in the tables may not always add up to the expected base.

In a number of questions, respondents were invited to give more than one answer: and so percentages may well add up to more than 100%.

Percentages are rounded to the nearest whole number. This may cause some mutually exclusive categories to sum to slightly more or slightly less than 100%.

Some sub-questions are filtered, that is, they are only asked of a proportion of respondents. Where questions are filtered, the base of relevant groups is indicated at the beginning of that table and percentages are derived from that base.

Regional analyses: inevitably, the number of sampling points in any one region is small. This fact should be taken into account when interpreting regional differences.

Analysis of weighted and unweighted samples

Sex, age, socio-economic grade

Base: All adults aged 17 or over	Unweighted		Weighted	
Total	5885	100%	4896	100%
Sex				
Male	2684	46	2381	49
Female	3201	54	2515	51
Age				
16-24	751	13	586	12
25-34	1015	17	887	18
35-44	1154	20	1,002	20
45-54	904	15	757	15
55+	2061	35	1663	34
Socio-economic grade				
AB	971	16	906	19
C1	1538	26	1398	29
C2	1275	22	1084	22
DE	2101	36	1509	31
Standard Region				
London	607	10	483	10
South East	914	16	695	14
South West	440	7	324	7
East Anglia	198	3	208	4
East Midlands	373	6	412	8
West Midlands	433	7	470	10
North West	541	9	586	12

Yorkshire and Humberside	469	8	515	11
North	309	5	344	7
Wales	995	17	241	5
Scotland	439	7	483	10
Northern Ireland	167	3	144	3

Regions

Standard Regions

1. Yorkshire/Humberside
2. North – Cumbria, Northumberland, Durham, Cleveland, Tyne and Wear
3. South West – Cornwall, Devon, Somerset, Dorset, Wiltshire, Gloucestershire
4. East Midlands – Northamptonshire, Leicestershire, Lincolnshire, Nottinghamshire, Derbyshire
5. South East – Essex, Hertfordshire, Bedfordshire, Buckinghamshire, Oxfordshire, Berkshire, Hampshire, Surrey, Sussex, Kent
6. East Anglia – Norfolk, Suffolk, Cambridgeshire
7. West Midlands – Hereford, Worcester, Shropshire, Staffordshire, Warwickshire
8. North West – Cheshire, Greater Manchester, Lancashire, Merseyside
9. Wales
10. Scotland
11. Greater London

Government Office Regions

1. Yorkshire/ Humberside
2. North East – Northumberland, Durham, Cleveland, Tyne and Wear
3. South West – Cornwall, Devon, Somerset, Dorset, Wiltshire, Gloucestershire
4. East Midlands – Northamptonshire, Leicestershire, Lincolnshire, Nottinghamshire, Derbyshire
5. South East – Buckinghamshire, Oxfordshire, Berkshire, Hampshire, Surrey, Sussex, Kent
6. Eastern – Norfolk, Suffolk, Cambridgeshire, Essex, Hertfordshire, Bedfordshire
7. West Midlands – Hereford, Worcester, Shropshire, Staffordshire, Warwickshire
8. North West – Cheshire, Greater Manchester, Lancashire, Merseyside, Cumbria
9. Wales
10. Scotland
11. Greater London

The questionnaire

Items marked "*" appear on the Welsh version only.

INTERVIEWER: PLEASE CODE AREA WHERE YOU ARE WORKING.

    01:   Wales
    02:   Rest of the country

(Route: if coded 01 ask Q.A. Others go to Q.1)

Q.A   For the next series of questions you have the opportunity of answering them in Welsh. The questions are on learning and education. If you would like to answer the questions in Welsh I will be happy to arrange for a Welsh-speaking interviewer to come and interview you at a time that is convenient. Would you like to answer the questions in Welsh, would you prefer to answer the questions in Welsh but would be prepared to answer them in English, or would you carry on answering in English?
    01:   Would like to answer questions in Welsh
    02:   Prefer Welsh but will answer in English
    03:   Will answer in English

(Route: if coded 01 go to Q.B. Others go to Q.1)

Q.B   Will it be okay, therefore, for a Welsh speaking interviewer to give you a call in the next couple of weeks to arrange for the interview to be carried out in Welsh?
    01:   Yes – acceptable
    02:   No – not acceptable

SHOW SCREEN

Q.1   Apart from television and radio, what are your main leisure time activities and interests?
    01:   Arts: painting, pottery, writing, photography etc.
    02:   Committee work\voluntary service
    03:   Gardening
    04:   Going to church\temple\mosque
    05:   DIY\handicrafts\woodwork
    06:   Indoor games including chess, bridge
    07:   Listening to music
    08:   Music as a performer
    09:   Physical activities and sports, including walking and keep fit
    10:   Reading
    11:   Sewing\knitting\making clothes\embroidery
    12:   Social activities (family, friends, disco, eating out, pub)
    13:   Other (please specify)
    (N)
    (DK)

SHOW SCREEN

Q.2   How often do you do any of the following?
- ...   Visit a public library
- ...   Go to the cinema
- ...   Go to the theatre
- ...   Go to a concert\opera\ballet
- ...   Go to a museum
- ...   Go to an art gallery
- ...   Go to a community centre\social club
- ...   Go to a place of worship

01:   Once a week or more often
02:   Less than once a week to once a month
03:   Less often\never
(DK)

I would now like to talk about the sort of learning that people do. Learning can mean practising, studying, or reading about something. It can also mean being taught, instructed or coached. This is so you can develop skills, knowledge, abilities or understanding of something. Learning can also be called education or training. You can do it regularly (each day or month) or you can do it for a short period of time. It can be full-time or part-time, done at home, at work, or in another place like college. Learning does not have to lead to a qualification. I am interested in any learning you have done, whether or not it was finished.

SHOW SCREEN

Q.3   Which of the following statements most applies to you?

01:   I am currently doing some learning activity now.
02:   I have done some learning activity in the last 3 years
03:   I have studied\learnt but it was over 3 years ago
04:   I have not studied\learnt since I left full time education
(DK)

(Route: If coded 01 or 02 at Q.3 go to Q.4a, others go to Q.16a)

Q.4a   What subjects are you learning about or have you most recently learnt about?
PROBE: anything else?
- 01:   Accountancy
- 02:   Arts: including painting\pottery\sculpture\design
- 03:   Basic maths\numeracy
- 04:   Basic skills: reading\writing\literacy
- 05:   Building trades
- 06:   Business studies\administration\management (including HR and marketing)
- 07:   Car maintenance
- 08:   Carpentry\DIY\Handicrafts
- 09:   Communication skills including customer care
- 10:   Computer skills\information technology\using the Internet
- 11:   Cookery\catering
- 12:   Dance
- 13:   Dressmaking\tailoring\needlecraft
- 14:   Driving (including HGV)
- 15:   Engineering (electronic\mechanical\construction)
- 16:   English as a second or additional language

17:   English language\literature
18:   Foreign languages (excluding Welsh)
19:   Gardening\horticulture\garden design\floristry
20:   Health and medicine: including nursing and first aid
21:   History\local history
22:   Law\bar exams
23:   Music
24:   Photography
25:   Religion\bible studies\theology
26:   Self development\assertiveness training
27:   Science\maths\statistics
28:   Shorthand\typing\office training
29:   Social sciences\psychology\sociology etc.
30:   Social work\social services\community care
31:   Sports\gymnastics\keep fit
32:   Welsh language
33:   Mother tongue, other than English or Welsh
34:   Other informal\community learning (including learning to learn) (type in)
35:   Other professional and vocational qualifications (type in)
36:   Other academic subjects (type in)
37:   Other 'leisure' subjects (type in)
(DK)

(Route: if more than one subject coded at Q.4a go to Q.4b. Others go to Q.5)

Q.4b   What is the main subject you are learning about or have most recently learnt about?
        (List of answers given at Q.4a)

Q.5   How did you find out about (INSERT SUBJECT)?
        PROBE: Any other ways?
        01:   Friends\family
        02:   Work mates\colleagues
        03:   Printed publicity (posters\leaflets etc) delivered to home
        04:   Printed publicity (posters\leaflets etc) elsewhere
        05:   Newspapers\magazines
        *29: Papur Bro
        06:   College: further education, tertiary, 6th form college
        07:   Adult education centre\evening institute\Workers' Educational Association
        08:   University\higher education institution\Open University
        09:   Community centre\voluntary organisation\religious group
        10:   School
        11:   Trade union\professional association
        12:   Public library
        13:   LSC (Learning and Skills Council), TEC (Training and Enterprise Council)\LEC ELWa
              (Education and Learning Wales)
        14:   SBS (Small Business Service), Chamber of Commerce, Business Connect, Scottish
              Enterprise
        15:   Work: my employer\training officer\personnel officer
        16:   Careers service\advice and guidance service\Connexions\Careers Wales
        17:   Job centre\Job club\UBO\employment service e.g. New Deal
        18:   Town hall\council offices
        19:   learndirect (including the University for Industry (UfI))
        20:   Other telephone helpline, including BBC
        21:   CAB (Citizen's Advice Bureau)\advice centre
        22:   Radio
        *30: Radio – Welsh medium

23: Television
*31: Television – Welsh medium
24: Internet\world wide web\online
25: GP\health centre\clinic
26: Health club\fitness club\leisure club\sports centre
27: Social worker\community outreach worker
28: Other (please specify)
(DK)

SHOW SCREEN

Q.6 On this screen there are some reasons people have given for why they choose to learn about a certain subject or skill. Thinking of your learning of (INSERT SUBJECT), which of the following best describe the reason you started this learning?
(Order of list randomised but 01 and 02 fixed in that order, and 16-19 fixed at bottom)
01: To get a job
02: To get a job with a different employer
03: To change the type of work I do
04: To get a recognised qualification
05: To help in my current job
06: To get a promotion
07: To get a rise in earnings
08: To make my work more satisfying
09: To help me get onto a future course of learning
10: To develop myself as a person
11: To improve my self-confidence
12: I enjoy learning\it gives me pleasure
13: I am interested in the subject\personal interest
14: To meet people
15: As a result of participating in another activity
16: Not really my choice – employer requirement
17: Not really my choice – professional requirement
18: Not really my choice – benefit requirement
19: Only type of learning available
(DK)

SHOW SCREEN

Q.7 Where is the main location that you do or did this learning?
01: Where I work
02: Employer's training centre
03: Other private training centre\conference centre\hotel
04: Job centre\job club\skill centre
05: Local ICT learning centre (e.g. learndirect\UKonline)
06: Adult education centre\evening institute\Workers' Educational Association class
07: Further education college\tertiary\6th form college
08: University\higher education institution\Open University
09: Local primary school
10: Local secondary school
11: Other educational institution
12: Public library
13: Community centre\leisure centre
14: With an informal group e.g. women's group, church etc.
15: Voluntary organisation e.g. pre-school learning alliance, U3A etc
16: Health\fitness\leisure centre\club

17:    While driving\travelling
18:    At home – structured correspondence course or open learning
19:    At home – informal learning\from a book
20:    At home – from radio\TV
21:    At home – using a computer, CD Rom, Internet
22:    Other (please specify)
(DK)

SHOW SCREEN

Q.8   How easy is it to get to where your learning takes or took place?
    01:    Don't or didn't have to travel: learn(t) at home\work
    02:    Very easy
    03:    Fairly easy
    04:    Fairly difficult
    05:    Very difficult
    (DK)

Q.9   Thinking about (INSERT SUBJECT), about how many hours a week do you or did you spend on learning?

SHOW SCREEN

Q.10   Thinking about (INSERT SUBJECT), how long do you expect to, or did you study for this altogether?
    01:    Less than 1 week
    02:    1 week – 1 month
    03:    Over 1 month – 3 months
    04:    Over 3 months – 6 months
    05:    7 – 12 months
    06:    Over 1 – 2 years
    07:    Over 2 years
    (DK)

SHOW SCREEN

Q.11a   What qualifications, if any, are (were if coded 02 at Q.3) you aiming towards?
    01:    None\not aiming for qualification
    02:    GCSE grades A*-C\SCE Credit Level Standard Grades
    03:    GCSE grades D-G\SCE Foundation Level Standard Grades
    04:    A level, A\S level, S level\AVCE\Scottish Highers
    20:    RSA
    21:    City and Guilds
    16:    Open College Network (OCN) Credit
    22:    BTEC\SCOTVEC\SCOTEV
    05:    Diploma in Higher Education (DipHE)
    06:    Foundation Degree
    07:    Degree (BA, BSc, BEd)
    08:    Higher degree (e.g. MA, MSc, PhD)
    09:    Nursing\medical\clinical qualification
    10:    PGCE or other teaching qualification
    11:    Modern Apprenticeship
    12:    NVQ\SVQ
    13:    GNVQ\GSVQ
    14:    ONC\OND

15:   HNC\HND
17:   Other post-graduate qualification (please specify)
18:   Other professional qualification (please specify)
19:   Other qualifications (please specify)
(DK)

(Route: if coded 02 or 03 at Q.11a ask Q.11b. Others see Q.11c)

Q.11b   How many GCSEs or SCEs are (were if coded 02 at Q.3) you aiming for?
(Type in box, allow 2 digits)
(DK)

(Route: if coded 20 at Q.11a ask Q.11c. Others see Q.11d)

SHOW SCREEN

Q.11c   What is (was if coded 02 at Q.3) the level of RSA you are (were if coded 02 at Q.3) aiming for?
01:   Higher Diploma
02:   Advanced Diploma or Certificate
03:   First Diploma
04:   Certificate
05:   Other RSA qualification (please specify)
(DK)

(Route: if coded 04 at Q.11a ask Q.11d. Others see Q.11e)

SHOW SCREEN

Q.11d   How many A, A\S, S levels, AVCEs or Scottish Highers are (were if coded 02 at Q.3) you aiming
for?
01:   -1-
02:   -2-
03:   -3-
04:    4 or more
(DK)

(Route: if coded 12 at Q.11a ask Q.11e. Others see Q.11f)

SHOW SCREEN

Q.11e   What is (was if coded 02 at Q.3) the level of NVQ\SVQ you are (were if coded 02 at Q.3) aiming
for?
01:   Level 5
02:   Level 4
03:   Level 3
04:   Level 2
05:   Level 1
06:   Units towards NVQ\SVQ
07:   Other NVQ (specify)
(DK)

(Route: if coded 13 at Q.11a ask Q.11f. Others see Q.11g)

SHOW SCREEN

Q.11f   What is (was if coded 02 at Q.3) the level of GNVQ\GSVQ you are (were if coded 02 at Q.3) aiming for?

         01:    Advanced
         02:    Intermediate
         03:    Foundation
         04:    Other GNVQ\QSVQ qualification (specify)
         (DK)

(Route: if coded 16 at Q.11a ask Q.11g. Others see Q.11h)

SHOW SCREEN

Q.11g   What is (was if coded 02 at Q.3) the level of OCN credit you are (were if coded 02 at Q.3) aiming for?

         02:    Level 3
         03:    Level 2
         04:    Level 1
         06:    Entry level
         05:    Other OCN qualification (specify)
         (DK)

(Route: if coded 21 at Q.11a ask Q.11h. Others see Q.11i)

SHOW SCREEN

Q.11h   What is (was if coded 02 at Q.3) the level of City and Guilds you are (were if coded 02 at Q.3) aiming for?

         01:    Part 3\Final\Advanced Craft
         02:    Part 2\Craft\Intermediate
         03:    Part 1
         04:    Other City and Guilds qualification (please specify)
         (DK)

(Route: if coded 22 at Q.11a ask Q.11i. Others go to Q.12)

SHOW SCREEN

Q.11i   What is (was if coded 02 at Q.3) the level of BTEC\SCOTVEC\SCOTEV you are (were if coded 02 at Q.3) aiming for?

         01:    Higher Certificate Diploma
         02:    National Certificate Diploma
         03:    First\General Diploma
         04:    First\General Certificate
         05:    Other BTEC\SCOTVEC\SCOTEV qualification (please specify)
         (DK)

SHOW SCREEN

Q.12   Did you complete your learning or course?

         01:    Yes, completed it
         02:    No, gave up before end
         03:    Still studying it
         (DK)

SHOW SCREEN

Q.13   Can you identify any changes or benefits that have happened as a result of your learning?

(Scripter: randomise order of list but fix 01 and 02 in that order)
01:    I have got\expect to get a job
02:    I have got\expect to get a job with a different employer
03:    I have changed\expect to change the type of work I do
04:    I have got\expect to get a recognised qualification
05:    I have been helped\expect to be helped in my current job
06:    I have got\expect to get a promotion or a rise in earnings
07:    My work has become\I expect my work to become more satisfying
08:    I have moved\expect to move onto a further course of learning
09:    I have developed myself as a person
10:    My self-confidence has improved
11:    I have met new people\made new friends
12:    My health has improved
13:    I enjoy learning more: more aware of the benefits of learning, know I can learn etc.
14:    My children\my family have become more interested in learning
15:    I am more involved in local events and issues
(DK)

SHOW SCREEN

Q.14   Who pays or paid the fees for this learning?
        PROBE: Who else?
01:    No fees to pay
02:    Myself
03:    Family\relative
04:    My employer\potential employer paid outside fees
05:    My employer funded provision of learning
06:    Government training scheme e.g. New Deal
07:    ILA (Individual Learning Account)
08:    Help from my institution e.g. access funds, bursaries etc.
08:    Local authority grant
09:    Other government funding
10:    Charitable trust or other non-government organisation
11:    Other (specify)
(DK)

SHOW SCREEN

Q.15   Sometimes learning can have other costs apart from fees. The following are some of the costs that
        people can experience when they do some learning. Thinking about your main learning of
        (INSERT SUBJECT), has it led or did it lead to any costs like these?
01:    No other costs
02:    Loss of wages\salary\overtime
03:    Loss of benefit(s)
04:    Cost of childcare
05:    Travel costs
06:    Costs of equipment (e.g. books\computers\Internet charges)
07:    Other (specify)
(DK)

SHOW SCREEN

Q.16a What is the highest level of examination or qualification that you now hold, including any that
       you may have gained since leaving full-time education?
       01:   No qualifications held
       02:   O level\CSE 1\Matriculation\School Certificate
       03:   GCSE grade A*-C\SCE Credit Level Standard Grade
       04:   GCSE grade D-G\SCE Foundation Level Standard Grade
       05:   A level, A\S level, S level, AVCE, Scottish Higher
       22:   RSA\Pitman's
       23:   City and Guilds
       18:   Open College Network (OCN) Credit
       24:   BTEC\SCOTVEC\SCOTEV
       06:   Diploma in Higher Education (DipHE)
       07:   Foundation Degree
       08:   Degree (BA, BSc, BEd)
       09:   Higher Degree (MA, MSc, PhD)
       11:   Nursing\medical\clinical qualification
       12:   PGCE or other teaching qualification
       13:   Apprenticeship\Modern Apprenticeship
       14:   NVQ\SVQ
       15:   GNVQ\GSVQ
       16:   ONC\OND
       17:   HNC\HND
       19:   Other post-graduate qualification (specify)
       20:   Other professional qualification (specify)
       21:   Other qualifications (please specify)
       (DK)

(Route: if coded 02 at Q.16a ask Q.16aa. Others see Q.16b)

SHOW SCREEN

Q.16aa How many subjects at O level\CSE grade 1\Matriculation\School Certificate do you hold?
        (Type in box, allow 2 digits)
        (DK)

(Route: if coded 03 at Q.16a ask Q.16b. Others see Q.16c)

SHOW SCREEN

Q.16b How many GCSE's grades A* to C, or SCE Credit Level Standard Grades, do you hold?
       01:   -1-
       02:   -2-
       03:   -3-
       04:   -4-
       05:   5 or more (type in)
       (DK)

(Route: if coded 04 at Q.16a ask Q.16c. Others see Q.16d)

SHOW SCREEN

Q.16c How many GCSE's grades D to G, or SCE Foundation Level Standard Grades, do you hold?
          01:   -1-
          02:   -2-
          03:   -3-
          04:   -4-
          05:   5 or more (type in)
          (DK)

(Route: if coded 05 at Q.16a ask Q.16d. Others see Q.16e)

SHOW SCREEN

Q.16d How many A levels, A\S levels, S levels, AVCEs, or Scottish Highers do you hold?
          01:   -1-
          02:   -2-
          03:   -3-
          04:   4 or more
          (DK)

(Route: if coded 14 at Q.16a ask Q.16e. Others go to Q.16f)

SHOW SCREEN

Q.16e What is the highest level of NVQ\SVQ you hold?
          01:   Level 5
          02:   Level 4
          03:   Level 3
          04:   Level 2
          05:   Level 1
          06:   Units towards NVQ\SVQ
          07:   Other NVQ (specify)
          (DK)

(Route: if coded 15 at Q.16a ask Q.16f. Others see Q.16g)

SHOW SCREEN

Q.16f What is the highest level of GNVQ\GSVQ you hold?
          01:   Advanced
          02:   Intermediate
          03:   Foundation
          04:   Other GNVQ\QSVQ qualification (specify)
          (DK)

(Route: if coded 18 at Q.16a ask Q.16g. Others see Q.16h)

SHOW SCREEN

Q.16g What is the highest level of OCN you hold?
          02:   Level 3
          03:   Level 2
          04:   Level 1
          06:   Entry level
          05:   Other OCN qualification (specify)
          (DK)

(Route: if coded 22 at Q.16a ask Q.16h. Others see Q.16i)

SHOW SCREEN

Q.16h   What is the highest level of RSA\Pitman's you hold?
      01:   Higher Diploma
      02:   Advanced Diploma or Certificate
      03:   First Diploma
      04:   Certificate
      05:   Other RSA\Pitman's qualification (please specify)
      (DK)

(Route: if coded 23 at Q.16a ask Q.16i. Others see Q.16j)

SHOW SCREEN

Q.16i   What is the highest level of City and Guilds you hold?
      01:   Part 3\Final\Advanced Craft
      02:   Part 2\Craft\Intermediate
      03:   Part 1
      04:   Other City and Guilds qualification (please specify)
      (DK)

(Route: if coded 24 at Q.16a ask Q.16j. Others go to Q.17)

SHOW SCREEN

Q.16j   What is the highest level of BTEC\SCOTVEC\SCOTEV you hold?
      01:   Higher Certificate Diploma
      02:   National Certificate Diploma
      03:   First\General Diploma
      04:   First\General Certificate
      05:   Other BTEC\SCOTVEC\SCOTEV qualification (please specify)
      (DK)

SHOW SCREEN

Q.17   How old were you when you finished full-time education?
      01:   14 or under
      02:   15
      03:   16
      04:   17
      05:   18
      06:   19
      07:   20
      08:   21
      09:   22
      10:   23
      11:   24
      12:   25 or more
      13:   Still a full-time student: school\college\university
      (DK)

SHOW SCREEN

Q.18   How likely are you to take up any learning in the next 3 years?
      01: Very likely
      02: Fairly likely
      03: Fairly unlikely
      04: Very unlikely
      (DK)

(Route: if coded 02 to 04 or DK at Q.18 go to Q.19. Others go to Q.20)

SHOW SCREEN

Q.19   From the following list what, if anything, would you say are the main things preventing you from learning these days?
PROBE: Anything else?
      01: Not interested\don't want to
      02: Cost\money\can't afford it
      03: Childcare arrangements\caring for others
      04: Transport\too far to travel
      05: Work\other time pressures
      06: I don't like being in groups of people I don't know
      07: I don't know what is available
      08: I feel I am too old
      09: I am too ill\too disabled
      10: I am worried about being out alone
      11: I haven't got round to doing it
      12: I feel no need to learn anymore
      13: I don't feel colleges\centres are welcoming
      14: I do not have the qualifications I need
      15: I do not have the abilities I need
      16: I am put off by tests and exams
      17: I am too nervous about the idea of starting learning
      18: I don't feel confident enough
      19: I would not be able to get time off work
      20: I've tried learning in the past and it has been unsuccessful
      21: No suitable courses are available
  * 24: Lack of opportunity to learn in Welsh
  * 25: Lack of opportunity to learn in other mother tongue
      22: Lack of opportunity to learn in other tongue
      23: Other (please specify)
      (N)
      (DK)

Q.20   What (else), if anything, would you be most interested in learning about if you could?
(List as Q.4a)

SHOW SCREEN

Q.21   I will now read out a list of statements people have made about different types of learning. For each one, please tell me how much you agree or disagree. So firstly, how much do you agree or disagree with
    ...   Learning is enjoyable for its own sake
    ...   I am confident about learning new skills
    ...   People who get training find their jobs are more interesting
    ...   People who get trained at work end up with better promotion or better pay
    ...   People should not be expected to learn new skills for their career in their own time
    ...   There is not enough help and advice available about the different sorts of learning people can do
    ...   I don't see why I should pay for learning that is to do with my job or career

    01:    Agree strongly
    02:    Agree
    03:    Neither agree nor disagree
    04:    Disagree
    05:    Disagree strongly
    (DK)

SHOW SCREEN

Q.22   I will now read two more statements and, again, for each one, please tell me how much you agree or disagree. So firstly, how much do you agree or disagree with
    ...   In general most people can be trusted
    ...   I am optimistic about my future
    01:    Agree strongly
    02:    Agree
    03:    Neither agree nor disagree
    04:    Disagree
    05:    Disagree strongly
    (DK)

SHOW SCREEN

Q.23   Which of the following statements, if any, applies to your recent or current situation?
    01:    I have started a family
    02:    I have lost my job\ been made redundant
    03:    I have started a new job\been promoted
    04:    I have taken early retirement\retired
    05:    I have been involved in a broken marriage\broken up with my partner
    06:    I have recently lost a partner\spouse
    07:    I have moved home\moved to a new area
    08:    I wanted\want promotion at work
    09:    I wanted\want to help my children learn
    10:    I had a serious illness
    11:    I have a new\increasing disability
    (N)
    (DK)

SHOW SCREEN

Q.24   Which, if any, of these had any bearing on your decision to take up learning?
    (List as at Q.23 filtered on answers at Q.23)

Q.25   Have you heard of the European Social Fund?
       PROBE: You may have heard of it as ESF?
       01:   Yes
       02:   No
       (DK)

(Route: if coded 01 at Q.25 ask Q.26. Others go to Q.27a)

Q.26   What do you think the European Social Fund does?
       PROBE: What else? PROBE: Anything else?

       (Open-ended)

SHOW SCREEN

Q.27a   Which of these do you have regular access to?
        PROBE: Any others?
        01:   Mobile phone
        02:   CD player
        03:   DVD player
        04:   Computer\PC\laptop
        05:   Internet via normal phone line
        06:   Internet via Broadband connection
        (N)
        (DK)

(Route: if 05 or 06 coded, go to Q.27b. Others go to Q.28)

SHOW SCREEN

Q.27b   Which of these activities have you ever used the Internet for?
        PROBE: Any others?
        01:   Using e-mail
        02:   Using chat rooms or sites
        03:   Finding information about goods and services (including holidays, flights, houses, etc.)
        04:   Buying or ordering tickets, goods or services (excluding shares and financial services)
        05:   Personal banking, financial and investment activities
        06:   Looking for jobs or work
        07:   Downloading software, including games
        08:   Playing or downloading music
        09:   Finding information related to children's schoolwork
        10:   Finding information for my learning\training
        11:   Learning on\off-line
        12:   Using or accessing government or official services
        13:   General browsing or surfing
        14:   Other things
        (N)
        (DK)

SHOW SCREEN

Q.27c And which of these activities do you mostly use the Internet for?
    01: Using e-mail
    02: Using chat rooms or sites
    03: Finding information about goods and services (including holidays,
         flights, houses, etc.)
    04: Buying or ordering tickets, goods or services (excluding shares and financial services)
    05: Personal banking, financial and investment activities
    06: Looking for jobs or work
    07: Downloading software, including games
    08: Playing or downloading music
    09: Finding information related to children's schoolwork
    10: Finding information for my learning\training
    11: Learning on\off-line
    12: Using or accessing government or official services
    13: General browsing or surfing
    14: Other things
    (N)
    (DK)

SHOW SCREEN

Q.28 People of different cultural backgrounds may have different needs in relation to studying and learning. With this in mind, can you tell me which of the following best describes you?
    01: White
    02: Black – Caribbean
    03: Black – African
    04: Black – British
    05: Black – other (please specify)
    06: Bangladeshi
    07: Indian
    08: Pakistani
    09: Chinese
    10: Asian – British
    11: Asian – other (specify)
    12: Arab
    13: Cypriot
    14: Other (specify)
    (R)

SHOW SCREEN

Q.29 What is your mother tongue, that is the language you first learned as a child?
    01: Arabic
    02: Bengali
    03: English
    04: Greek
    05: Gujarati
    06: Hindi
    07: Punjabi
    08: Somali
    13: Turkish
    09: Urdu
    10: Yemeni

11:   Welsh
12:   Other (specify)
(DK)

SHOW SCREEN

Q.30   Through which language do you prefer to learn?
     01:   Arabic
     02:   Bengali
     03:   English
     04:   Greek
     05:   Gujarati
     06:   Hindi
     07:   Punjabi
     08:   Somali
     13:   Turkish
     09:   Urdu
     10:   Yemeni
     11:   Welsh
     12:   Other (specify)
     (DK)